THE BOXERS OF WALES

Volume 4: Swansea & Llanelli

GARETH JONES

St David's Press
Cardiff

Published in Wales by St. David's Press, an imprint of

Ashley Drake Publishing Ltd
PO Box 733
Cardiff
CF14 2YX

www.st-davids-press.com

First Impression – 2015

ISBN 978-1-902719-45-0

© Ashley Drake Publishing Ltd 2015
Text © Gareth Jones 2015

The right of Gareth Jones to be identified as the author of this work has been asserted in accordance with the Copyright Design and Patents Act of 1988.

All rights reserved. No part of this publication may be reproduced, stored in a retrieval system, or transmitted, in any form or by any means without the prior permission of the publishers.

British Library Cataloguing-in-Publication Data.
A CIP catalogue for this book is available from the British Library.

Contents

Acknowledgements	iv	Colin JONES	84
Foreword	v	Ken JONES	93
Introduction	vi	Randy JONES	95
		John KAIGHIN	98
Teddy BARROW	1	Barrie KELLEY	100
Len BEYNON	4	Jack KILEY	102
Jeff BURNS	7	Dean LYNCH	105
Carlo COLARUSSO	9	Enzo MACCARINELLI	107
Mike COPP	12	Miguel MATTHEWS	115
Brian CURVIS	14	Terry MATTHEWS	117
Cliff CURVIS	20	Frank McCORD	120
Ken CURVIS	25	Ross McCORD	123
Gipsy DANIELS	27	Neville MEADE	125
Glynne DAVIES	32	Damian OWEN	130
Shon DAVIES	35	Keith PARRY	133
Robert DICKIE	38	Geoff PEGLER	136
Dave GEORGE	43	Dean PHILLIPS	139
Don GEORGE	46	Delme PHILLIPS	142
Neil HADDOCK	49	Petrina PHILLIPS	145
Nigel HADDOCK	53	Ray PRICE	148
Ceri HALL	56	Chris WARE	151
Michael HARRIS	59	Tobias WEBB	153
Peter HARRIS	62	Jim WILDE	156
Floyd HAVARD	67	Jason WILLIAMS	159
Gareth HOWELLS	71	Taffy WILLIAMS	162
Chris JACOBS	73		
Doug JAMES	76	Supporting Cast	165
Ronnie JAMES	79	Bibliography	169

ACKNOWLEDGEMENTS

This volume of *The Boxers of Wales* has been strikingly different to others in the series. By some generational fluke, a large percentage of the fighters eligible for inclusion are of fairly recent vintage and, happily, still with us.

This has meant it has been possible to talk to many of the subjects. They have been unfailingly helpful, not merely in confirming or correcting my increasingly hazy memories, but in providing photos of their exploits. Families and friends of those long gone have been equally willing to supply background detail and to allow the use of treasured pictures.

I am particularly grateful to the editor of the *South Wales Evening Post*, Jonathan Roberts, for permission to use photographs and, similarly, recent editors of *Boxing News*. I must also acknowledge the generosity of those professional snappers who have contributed, notably the Huw Evans Picture Agency (www.huwevansimages.com), Peter Westall, Jane Warburton, Phil Sharkey and Kris Agland, along with David Roake (www.fightersFOTOS.co.uk).

Numerous others have smoothed the occasionally rocky paths of research. They include the staff at Cardiff Central, Swansea and Llanelli libraries, general secretary Rob Smith and his colleagues at the British Boxing Board of Control, members of the governing body's Welsh Area Council and its secretary, Mark Warner, and John Waith, of the Welsh Amateur Boxing Association.

There have been many individuals who have given time and effort to assist in the enterprise, tracking down ex-boxers and providing invaluable information. Among them I pay special tribute to Jim and Joanne Bromfield, Paul Boyce, Trevor Russell, Wynford Jones and Ronnie Morris and beg the forgiveness of those I have overlooked.

One name must again be at the top of the bill: that of Harold Alderman, MBE. His dedication to compiling old-timers' records and readiness to share the fruits of his labours make things a lot easier for those of us attempting to preserve the exploits of the men who thrilled us within the ropes.

FOREWORD

You know that scene in *Rocky II* where the local kids chase after him when he goes for a run? I was like that as a youngster. Alan and Mike Copp lived across the road when I was a boy and when they went sprinting up Townhill, all us lads would try to keep up with them – for a bit, anyway.

My Irish dad was a big fight fan and his enthusiasm rubbed off. My mate and I had one pair of gloves – I wore the right and he had the left – and we used to pretend to throw punches. Once I caught him in the face and, despite my instant apologies, he thumped me under the ribs. I promptly threw up over his father's car!

A classmate at school, Ian Lynch, used to go to the gym – his brothers, Paul and Dean, were both pros – and I decided to give it a try, heading for Gwent ABC and the inimitable Terry Grey. I trained there for a couple of months, but soon realised I lacked that special mentality a boxer needs.

The following year I was picked for Swansea Schools and from then on football took over, but I have never lost my love of the ring. I remember the thrill at an end-of-season awards ceremony at the Brangwyn Hall when I discovered the medals were being handed out by British heavyweight champion Neville Meade.

When I was with the Swans I went to shows at the Top Rank Suite and I used to know the likes of Rocky Reynolds, Kevin Roper, Ray Price and Geoff Pegler. And even though I've lived in England for the past 25 years I still keep in touch, celebrating from afar as Enzo Maccarinelli became Swansea's first world champion.

There have been so many great boxers from my home town – and from that place across the Loughor Bridge. This book tells their stories.

Chris Coleman
National Coach, Football Association of Wales

INTRODUCTION

It is hardly surprising that West Wales's urban heartland has provided so many champions. Physically demanding industries such as coal, tin and copper bred strong men with a fiercely competitive streak. But the laws that restrict their combative natures to a socially acceptable form also emerged from the area.

The Queensberry Rules were published in 1867. They outlawed "wrestling and hugging" and introduced such features as three-minute rounds with one-minute intervals, 10-second counts and an appropriately sized ring, all still part of boxing today. But although known by the name of the Marquess who endorsed them, they were drafted by a Welshman.

Eton-educated John Graham Chambers was born in Llanelly House, the son of a local landowner. And his sporting CV was exceptional. A champion walker, he also rowed for Cambridge and went on to coach four winning Boat Race crews, while wielding the oars in the support boat when Capt. Matthew Webb became the first person to swim the English Channel.

But it was as an administrator that he made the biggest impact, instituting championships in athletics, cycling, billiards and wrestling. Yet it is his gift to pugilism that is his greatest legacy and earned him election to the International Boxing Hall of Fame in 1990.

Chambers died in 1883, within weeks of his 40th birthday, but would have been proud of the number of his neighbours who have found success in the ring. He may even have known bare-knuckle bruisers like Swansea pair James Warner and William Samuels, although they were inclined to the sort of excesses his new regulations were intended to curtail.

But if there is a grandstand on the Elysian Fields from which past generations keep an eye on the sportsmen of later years, he will surely have raised a glass or two of nectar as fellow-townsman Gipsy Daniels flattened Max Schmeling inside a round, commiserated as those heroes from across the Loughor, Ronnie James, Brian Curvis, Colin Jones and Floyd Havard, vainly challenged the planet's best and finally cheered Enzo Maccarinelli to the echo as he brought a world champion's belt home to Swansea.

I hope this book will help modern readers appreciate what a rich fighting heritage was born of this comparatively small part of Wales, while saluting the brave boxers who created it.

GARETH JONES
August 2015

TEDDY BARROW
(1934–1988)

Welsh Middleweight Challenger 1957

The lad from Swansea's Townhill never wanted to be a boxer. A useful footballer who once had a trial with Arsenal, he would have preferred to earn a crust that way. But his father had other ideas.

Eddie Barrow was a hard man, who insisted his sons went into the ring. The younger, Len, loved it, but big brother Teddy, a gentler soul who hated the idea of deliberately hurting anyone, laced up the gloves without enthusiasm. It was ironic, therefore, that he proved so good at the sport.

Representing the Empire club founded by former star Jackie Kiley, the older Barrow boy won a Welsh youth title and a British Army Cadets championship before graduating to senior level and national honours at featherweight, outpointing defending champion Terry Andrews, from Treharris, in the 1952 final. Outpointed in the British semi-finals by the outstanding RAF ace, Percy Lewis, he was nevertheless urged to keep in training ahead of the Helsinki Olympics. But the call never came.

There were more trophies during National Service in the Royal Welch Fusiliers, but with demob came a day job with British Gas and a plunge into the world of professional boxing.

His new career began with a string of victories, notably a scintillating performance to hand a first defeat in 11 fights to Brummie Ken Barley at Willenhall, and a Liverpool Stadium debut which brought an ovation from the hard-bitten locals following his win

Teddy Barrow

over Yorkshireman Trevor Sykes, accompanied by rave notices about his straight left, likened by one observer to "an adder's tongue".

Those watching included local manager Tony Vairo, who signed Barrow when he returned to Merseyside to outpoint Bobby Gill a few months later. Still that splendid left lead continued to impress new audiences, on home ground in Cardiff and Carmarthen, as well as the punters of Blackpool, where he outclassed useful Londoner Ron Richardson. But disaster was lying in wait.

Cardiff welter Andy Andrews was hardly a household name even in the capital. And the first two rounds at Abergavenny did nothing to suggest an upset. But Barrow, after 15 straight successes, was not to add another; a moment's carelessness in the third allowed the blond Andrews to fire over a big right, which spun Teddy around and scrambled his senses. Grabbing the moment, Andy stormed in and floored the Swansea man three times before the referee jumped in.

Determined to erase the memory, Teddy was back in action 11 days later – no mandatory suspensions in those days – and had to climb off the floor in the first before repeating his victory over East Ender Richardson. But that was to prove his last success, as a career that had promised so much went rapidly downhill, not helped by his connections' insistence that he stayed at welter.

There was no disgrace in losing on points in Liverpool to unbeaten local Tommy Molloy, on his march to the British throne, but more significant in Welsh terms was an eight-round defeat to reigning 10st 7lb champion Rees Moore, although the Carmarthen crowd booed the verdict loud and long. When Scottish titleholder Jimmy Croll halted Barrow in five back in Liverpool, the Swansea stylist stepped away from the ring for seven months.

When he reappeared it was as a middleweight. But a points loss against Abertillery-born Midlander Freddie Cross at Streatham suggested it would not be the solution to all his problems. The Welsh Area Council, seeking to replace the retired Roy Agland on the middleweight throne, nevertheless ordered the pair to meet again to fill the vacancy.

A packed house at Sophia Gardens Pavilion on January 16, 1957, saw Cross dominant in what was his first appearance in his native land. His agility and fast fists built an early lead, although Teddy was able to drive him back for a time with a two-fisted attack in the seventh. But Freddie seemed headed for a points victory when the boom was lowered in the penultimate session.

A short right sent Barrow sprawling; he started to rise at three, thought better of it, and took another six seconds' rest. But his senses were not fully restored when the action resumed and there were two more counts of nine before North Walian referee Billy Jones saved him from his own bravery.

There was little left. Wolverhampton's George Roe knocked him out inside five minutes and then Cardiff-Trinidadian Eddie Bee added injury to insult at Cross Keys: he floored Barrow twice in the second and again in the fourth, but this time stumbled and fell across Teddy's legs. When the count was complete, fight doctor Jack Matthews, the Wales rugby legend, informed Teddy that he had a broken ankle!

There was one more chapter in the story. Barrow and Bee came together again at Porthcawl just over a year later. Eddie won inside two rounds and brought Teddy's career to a close. Newly married to Barbara, he finally turned his back on the ring and joined the Swansea Male Choir.

There was a spell in the fire service, whose medical revealed a life-long heart murmur that would have ruled out a boxing licence today, before a switch to maintenance work for British Steel at Trostre.

Teddy died of a heart attack at a dance, shortly before the birth of his first grandchild. Today Scott Barrow is what his grandfather wanted to be: a professional footballer with Newport County.

LEN BEYNON
(1912–1992)

- **Welsh Bantamweight Champion 1932–33, 1934, 1936–37**
- **Welsh Featherweight Champion 1936–42**

Few boxers can have appeared as regularly at one venue as Len Beynon. In a period of eight and a half years, he boxed at the Mannesmann Hall no fewer than 59 times, losing only five. As well as British opponents, the small shed, made of wood and corrugated iron, perched above the River Tawe opposite the Mannesmann tube works, saw him face travellers from as far afield as Cuba and Singapore; he even defeated Al Capone there, though this one came, not from Chicago, but the mean streets of Hartlepool.

Beynon was born in Barry, where his father, Charles, was a PTI to the local police, and his introduction to combat came from a simple reluctance to wear a hat. Back in the 1920s, going bare-headed was almost a revolutionary act and young Len found himself the target of many a derisory comment as he walked the streets. Fisticuffs tended to follow.

A move to Swansea saw Len turn pro at 17, making progress swift enough to see him matched with George Morgan, of the Tirphil fighting family, in a Welsh flyweight eliminator at Ammanford. A 15-round decision led to a shot at the vacant title in his home city's Shaftesbury Theatre on March 7, 1931. But his rival, former holder Freddie Morgan, went off like a train, throwing Beynon out of his stride and instilling a defensive mindset in the teenager, who was duly outpointed.

Len was turfed out for low blows in another eliminator, against Cliff Peregrine, but his only other losses before turning 20 came on points against class men: future British lightweight king Dave Crowley, reigning world fly champion Young

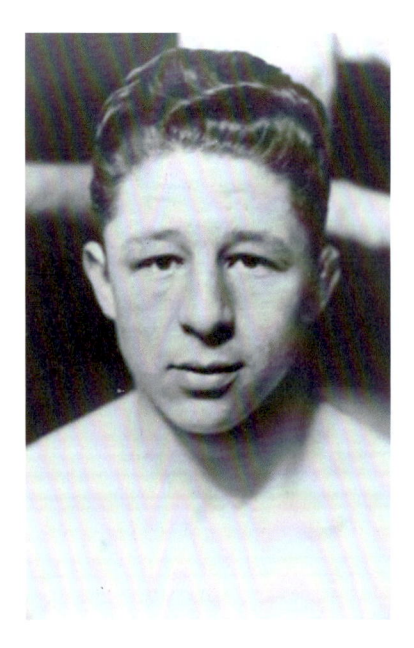

Len Beynon

Perez and his fellow-Frenchman, former world bantam boss Eugène Huat, and Manchester's Jackie Brown, at the time European titleholder and later to dethrone Perez.

Having grown into a bantam, he climbed between the ropes on June 11, 1932, to challenge Welsh ruler Terence Morgan, brother of old foe George. Len had outpointed the Tirphil man in a non-title set-to in London and repeated the feat at Merthyr Labour Club, gradually imposing himself on a below-par holder, drawing Morgan's leads and countering effectively to the body.

Len won his next 16 on the trot to earn a British title eliminator against Scottish champion Willie Vint at Llanelli Working Men's Club. Many valley fans – and Beynon's London-based manager, Ted Broadribb – were unable to attend as a blizzard disrupted rail and road links. Len needed three attempts to make the weight, but was too strong for the shorter-armed Scot and forced a stoppage in the 13th. The Board promptly matched Beynon with former conqueror Crowley at the Blackfriars Ring, but this time Len let Crowley march forward throughout, keeping his left in the Londoner's face to emerge a close, but clear winner.

He still faced a final eliminator against former British bantam boss Dick Corbett on September 11, 1933, at the Vetch Field. Corbett, with the longer reach, took the opening rounds, but Beynon seemed to solve the problem. Both were cut, but Len finished strongly and many in the 7,000 crowd considered he had done enough. The referee, however, thought differently.

Two months later Beynon was no longer even Welsh champion, though his defeat by Treherbert's George 'Watt' Williams at the Mannesmann Hall on November 4, 1933, sparked huge controversy. The more experienced Williams had the upper hand inside, taking him in front after six rounds, but Beynon began mixing uppercuts and hooks with the stylish boxing. After a toe-to-toe last session, referee Will Bevan raised Williams's hand and fans stormed forward to protest. Women were lifted into the ring for safety and it was half an hour before order was restored.

Len had to wait 18 months to earn his revenge, comfortably outpointing Williams in a rematch and again receiving the call for a British eliminator, this time against dethroned champion Johnny King, who avenged two previous defeats with a points verdict.

Forced back to domestic matters, Beynon opted for a defence in Merthyr against Rhondda boy Mog Mason, whom he had also beaten twice. But their mutual dislike resulted in a brawl which eventually saw Len disqualified. Such an unsatisfactory outcome demanded another meeting, but it was 15 months before they faced each other once more, on February 6, 1936, at the old Mannesmann. This time Len concentrated on his skills, outboxing Mog from start to finish.

The belt was back in Swansea – and it was soon to be joined by another. Beynon stepped up to take on Welsh feather champion Stan Jehu on June 8, 1936, outspeeding and outjabbing the Maesteg man to gain a wide decision and become the first man to hold both titles simultaneously.

Beynon could still make bantam and travelled to Manchester to face former world ruler Jackie Brown in a British final eliminator, but while Len's left hand picked up early points, Brown's tornado-like attacks forced the Welshman back and clinched the honours.

Back at nine stone, Beynon was being stalked by a familiar figure: old bantam rival Williams had also put on a few pounds and challenged Len for the new crown. But the holder's brilliant left hand controlled the contest and even a controversial knockdown in the ninth did not affect the outcome. 'Georgie Watt' was soon back for another try, but by the seventh was taking enough punishment for his cornermen to toss in the towel.

Beynon now focussed on repelling invaders from beyond Wales, losing only once in 1938 – and that on points at the Vetch against a former world king and future Hall of Famer, Cincinnati southpaw Freddie Miller. Two reigning British champions visited the Mannesmann Hall within three weeks – bantam boss King and recently crowned feather ruler Jim 'Spider' Kelly – and were each seen off.

When war broke out Beynon signed up for the Royal Artillery and, despite an accident involving disinfectant which saw him suffer burns to the face, he boxed on, still winning most, but losing a few when careless punches prompted disqualification.

Released from the Army for essential war work as a shipwright, and later as a boilermaker, Len's ring career came to an anti-climactic close in 1942, when he and opponent Jackie Rankin were both thrown out for excessive clinching. It was hardly the finale deserved by one of Wales's best boxers of his era.

JEFF BURNS
(1948–)

🥊 Welsh Middleweight Challenger 1973

The man they called 'Bulldog' fell in love with boxing as a seven-year-old in Waun Wen, woken by his fight-fan father to listen to radio commentary on a Rocky Marciano bout. But it was only after he left Dynevor School at 15 to join the Royal Navy that he began to practise the sport in earnest.

It paid off with a brace of Navy junior titles and after leaving the service he earned a Welsh vest while representing three different Swansea amateur clubs. He turned pro in 1972 with Llanelli-based Glynne Davies and it was a successful venture, at least to begin with, as debut foe Dave Barrett was floored twice and cut before being pulled out at the end of the first round. There followed two points decisions and a stoppage of Dave Nelson in his Wolverhampton backyard. But just 12 days later, Jeff came a cropper.

Well ahead on points going into the final session in front of his hometown fans at the Top Rank Suite, Burns walked on to a big right from journeyman Londoner Billy Brooks and it was all over. Just as soon as his mandatory suspension had ended, Jeff was back in with the Chiswick man at the Glen Ballroom, Llanelli, taking the spoils after a small-hall thriller, helped by the presence in his corner of the legendary Howard Winstone.

Another former champion was involved in Jeff's training for much of his career. Following a falling-out between Davies and promoter Eddie Richards, Brian Curvis took over managerial duties, with Dickie Dobbs as his trainer, although there were no great tactical changes. As a 5ft 5in middleweight, Burns's battle plan was dictated by necessity. There was no way he could expect to outjab his taller opponents, so he focussed on crouching even lower in a bid to get inside. There, he could do some damage.

It was how he beat Les Avoth, scoring to the body often enough to eclipse the Cardiffian's success at distance. But he was suffering recurrent hand problems

Jeff Burns

and there was a further setback when late substitute Mike McCluskie was adjudged to have done enough in Jeff's next outing.

Burns had his arm raised against Liverpool's highly rated Ronnie Hough and lanky Crewe boy Pat Brogan, but in between suffered his first early loss. Llantwit Major's Clive Collins, who had beaten Jeff as an amateur, but lost to him in his pro bow, won the decider at Tonyrefail when a cut eyelid brought a fifth-round finish.

The Swansea man had already been matched to dispute the vacant Welsh middle title with old foe McCluskie in Haverfordwest, but it was postponed and switched to more familiar surroundings at the Top Rank. It made little difference: after a gruelling affair, fought mainly at close quarters, McCluskie, a bookbinder from Caerau, landed a solid left as Burns moved in and although the local fighter regained his feet he was counted out midway through the eighth round.

There was to be no further opportunity, although there was a third meeting with McCluskie. This time it was Jeff who answered a late call to arms at the National Sporting Club, but a vicious right dropped him in the fourth and his legs betrayed him as he rose, prompting referee Benny Caplan to end it.

The Burns career was in decline. A stoppage loss against ex-amateur star Tony Byrne saw him leave Curvis and rejoin Davies, but the results did not improve. When Southend's Mick Hussey, who had just been knocked out in 15 seconds, including the count, by Cardiffian Vaughan Innocent, bounced back to left-hook Jeff into unconsciousness, it prompted the loser to take a break from the ring.

There was a brief comeback in 1976, but a three-round defeat at the hands of future British light-middle champion Jimmy Batten provided the definitive full stop. Burns no longer had the enthusiasm for training and knew that, with his high-risk style, entering the ring less than fully fit was a recipe for disaster.

A bar manager at the much-missed Dolphin Hotel, he was a long-time union official and became the GMB's full-time regional officer a few months after quitting the ring.

CARLO COLARUSSO
(1970–   )

- Welsh Light-Middleweight Champion 1991–95
- British Middleweight Challenger 1995

Just as he was getting used to being champion of his native land, a letter arrived claiming he owed allegiance to another country. It almost wrecked his career in the ring.

Carlo Colarusso was one of 11 children born to a couple from Avellino who had settled in Wales. His father, Giovanni, worked down the pit by day and moonlighted as a barber to pay the bills that came with such a family. For some reason – they had never done it before – his parents decided to register his birth in Italy as well as in Britain. And when he turned 21, the authorities there wanted him back to do his national service.

Such a dilemma was far from the mind of the 12-year-old Carlo when he was first taken to Trostre ABC by his big brother. Michael was useful, twice reaching Welsh ABA finals, but his sibling soon surpassed him. A string of national age-group honours were followed by a senior crown in 1989, although the British final brought a one-round defeat by Midlander Neville Brown. The pair would cross gloves again.

It was time to try the pro ranks. The stocky youngster signed with local manager Hywel 'Cass' Davies, with amateur trainer Gareth Howells calling the shots in the gym. A stoppage win on his debut was a good start – even if officialdom was less pleased with his occasional war whoops during the action – but three defeats in a row dented his self-belief.

Things changed for Colarusso when he halted Kevin Hayde at the capital's STAR Centre. The Cardiffian was also promoting the dinner show,

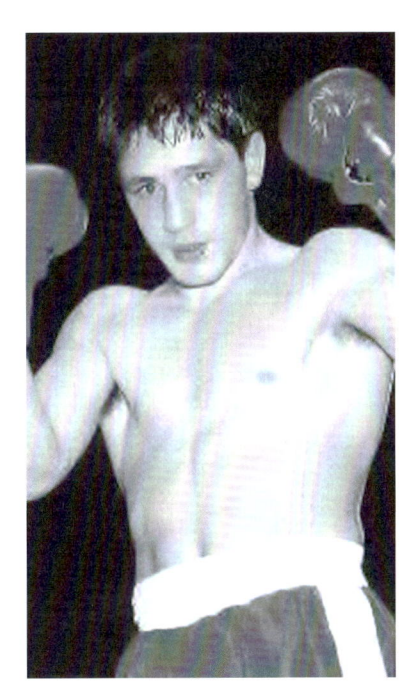

Carlo Colarusso

9

but within a round, his nose was broken; after three one-sided sessions, manager Dai Gardiner pulled Kevin out and he was able to return to his administrative duties.

It set Colarusso on a winning streak, including what another Cardiff fighter, Gary Pemberton, considered a premature stoppage. The Welsh Area Council ordered a rematch for the vacant Welsh light-middle throne and they came together on January 24, 1991, at Penyrheol Leisure Centre, on a debut promotion by Llanelli builder and farmer Les Cooper.

This time Carlo ended matters in the eighth – and once again the Pemberton camp were livid. Not at Ivor Bassett's intervention, but the fact that the Rhondda referee should have disqualified Colarusso two rounds earlier, when the Llanelli man plunged on top of his fallen foe and landed three punches as they lay on the canvas. Mr Bassett, later to have surgery to remove cataracts, somehow never saw what was clear to everyone else in the hall.

The incident overshadowed a cracking contest which saw Carlo decked and fortunate to survive the fifth, but taking over to floor the taller Pemberton in the seventh and complete the job in the next session.

Then those call-up papers landed on the doormat. Colarusso ignored them, not least because he spoke no Italian and had a baby son to look after. But he knew he could face arrest if he visited the country, so – apart from a family

Carlo's big chance

funeral spent half-expecting an official tap on the shoulder – he stayed clear until he was over the age limit.

Meanwhile, back in the ring, he wanted to bring boxing back to his home town, where there had been no promotions for nearly 20 years, and took on Swansea trier Russell Washer at the Bowls Centre. Washer's courage and durability were all that kept him on his feet until the referee's fifth-round intervention.

Carlo caused former world champion Lloyd Honeyghan a few scares at the Albert Hall, before being stopped on a cut, and then lasted the course with a global ruler-in-waiting in Richie Woodhall. Another future WBC king, Glenn Catley, was handed his first pro defeat in five rounds at the STAR; the Bristol boy never came to grips with the wide swings and looping hooks of the barrel-chested 'Welsh-Italian Stallion' and was dropped by a left before referee Wynford Jones stepped in.

It was almost a year before Colarusso boxed again and, surprisingly, it was a shot at the British champion up at middleweight, his amateur nemesis, Neville Brown. The Burton man completed a fourth successful defence on March 3, 1995, at the York Hall, a big right hand flattening Carlo in the seventh. Referee Dave Parris examined him as he rose and decided he was too groggy to continue.

The challenger had enjoyed his moments of success, roughing Brown up on the inside; the taller Midlander had the skill and accuracy, but things were tight enough for Mr Parris to have had the pair level after six, which did nothing to soothe Colarusso's feelings at what he viewed as an unwarranted ending.

By the end of the year the Llanelli man's career was over. An explosive first-round dismissal by unbeaten prospect Howard Eastman prompted him to call it a day.

There was the suggestion of a comeback at 31, abandoned when a sparring session with heavyweight John Davison left him with damaged ribs, and he focussed on helping his old mentor at the Trostre gym. Today, despite the demands of a young family, he is still available for emergency corner duty if the call comes.

MIKE COPP
(1956–)

🥊 Welsh Welterweight Challenger 1968

As a youngster, Michael was always in the shadow of big brother Alan. He reached a British junior final himself, but opted to turn pro with Eddie Richards at 19, while his sibling was still en route to his third Welsh ABA title.

There were two defeats to start, although fans at Croydon booed the decision in favour of Mick Minter, brother of Alan, and those at the National Sporting Club threw in "nobbings" after a thriller in which Abingdon debutant Peter Neal – later to challenge Colin Jones in the Eisteddfod Pavilion at Gowerton – stopped Mike just six seconds before the final bell.

Back on home ground at the Mayfair Suite, Copp halted Londoner Russ Shaw to start a run of five straight wins, including one on a Cardiff show that also featured the pro debuts of both brother Alan and future manager Colin Breen.

The run came to an end at the Rhondda Sports Centre against Cardiffian Chris Davies, whose controversial (and temporary) selection for the British Olympic squad managed by his father had prompted Alan, who had beaten him in the Welsh final, to turn pro in disgust.

The brothers were on opposite sides of some controversial refereeing at the Top Rank, where Cardiffian Joe Morgan handed Alan a dubious decision and counted out Mike when he seemed able to continue. In fairness to the official, Mike had already been floored once by Nigerian-born former Aberystwyth student Roysie Francis and there was confusion between him and trainer Dickie Dobbs over when to rise from the second knockdown.

His next outing in Wales also brought an early defeat, but no surprise. The fifth-round winner was Colin Jones, in the first appearance of a pro career which took him to three world title shots.

Unlucky to get no more than a draw against Central Area champion Terry Petersen in Doncaster, Mike had proved he was worthy to contest a belt of his own. The

Mike Copp

Welsh welterweight throne was empty and Copp was matched with Cardiffian Horace McKenzie to decide a new occupant in one of three title fights on Eddie Thomas's Afan Lido bill on July 10, 1978.

It must be admitted that the clash was less than riveting and referee Jim Brimmell lectured the pair repeatedly in an effort to draw out some more action. As it was, much of the excitement arrived in the intervals. After the bell to end the second, McKenzie

Mike Copp has debut-making Colin Jones covering up

landed the best shot of the fight, while a torrid close-quarter exchange came similarly late in the fourth. Horace finished strongly to make sure of the 99-94 verdict.

Brother Alan had already hung up his gloves after just five fights – four wins and a draw – but Mike battled on for another two years.

He lost in three rounds to future British light-middle champion Prince Rodney and was outpointed by future another who fought for the Lonsdale Belt, Albert Hillman. When his run of defeats reached seven he called it a day, becoming a manager and trainer with a gym at the back of his Sandfields home.

BRIAN CURVIS
(1937–2012)

- Empire Welterweight Champion 1960–1966
- British Welterweight Champion 1960–1966
- World Welterweight Challenger 1964
- European Welterweight Challenger 1966
- Empire Games Bronze Medallist 1958

More than two thousand people forced their way into Jack Solomons's gym in London's Great Windmill Street to watch the pair weigh in: Emile Griffith, the welterweight champion of the world, and a curly-headed kid from Swansea's Townhill. Many in the crowd were bedecked in black and gold silk bows that must have reminded the champion of the New York hat factory in which he worked outside the ring. For Brian Curvis, they were a link with a production line of a different kind.

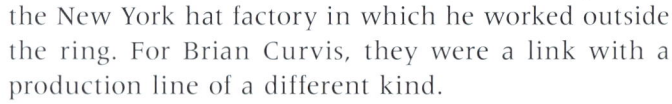

The colours were those of Swansea Premier Amateur Athletic Club, founded by his father, Dai, in an old stable loft. In these homely surroundings, Brian became the fourth son to undergo the unrelenting regime laid down by a man who had created numerous champions and was determined to find another among his own offspring. The ambitions vested in Dai's eldest sons had been shattered by the war; the other two were to fulfill their father's dreams, although Brian, the youngest by 10 years, achieved fame too late for it to be enjoyed by the old man.

His baby cut a swathe through all opposition. Schoolboy and junior titles in every age group were followed by success as a senior, but Dai, alas, died before the Welsh ABA welter title was won in 1958. A week later Cpl B. Nancurvis – now a National Serviceman with

Brian Curvis

the RAOC, the full surname betraying his family's Cornish roots – took the Army crown and in due course the British ABA championship. It was the year of the Empire Games in Cardiff, and Welsh fans were anticipating great things from the youngster. They were to be frustrated.

Brian boxed for Wales against West Germany in March, but the Games squad would not be named until the end of June. England, however, chose in May, and as Curvis was based there they invited him to join them. Thinking about the respective merits of birds in hand and in bushes, he agreed.

The night Brian won his first title

So it was in a white singlet that he outpointed a bald Australian, Johnny Fitzpatrick, to earn a bronze medal. South African Joe Greyling prevented any further progress; probably just as well, as the sight of him winning gold for England might have been hard for the Welsh fans to take. Now, it was time to turn pro.

Brian merely wanted to add enough to his earnings as a press operator to buy a second-hand car. A two-round debut win and Brian's ambitions grew: maybe he should carry on until he got beaten, and by then perhaps a brand-new motor would not be out of the question. That first defeat was not to come around for another three years, when he was already a double champion.

Brother Cliff had taken charge of Brian's career and believed in regular work. There were 13 victories in 10 months, and they created quite an impression. A new promoter called Mickey Duff wanted Curvis to meet Bootle's Tony Smith in a British final eliminator, but Cliff was looking beyond such domestic concerns. He was already aiming at the world champion, Don Jordan. But even Jack Solomons could not persuade Jordan to travel for a non-title fight. Instead George Barnes, a banana farmer from New South Wales, was offered £7,000 to venture across to old South Wales and place his Empire crown on the line. The Australian was 33, and had held the title off and on for the past six years, but few among the 14,000 who thronged to the Vetch Field on May 9, 1960, had any doubts that youth would be served.

Equally confident was Ted Broadribb, the old head brought in to guide the young fists. He left Curvis to do his own thing for the first five rounds, in which the suntanned champion succeeded in raising a slight swelling beneath the Welshman's right eye. Then he introduced the strategy that was to steal the title. For the first half of each round, Brian was to do nothing more than defend himself; then Broadribb would tap the canvas, and the challenger should turn up the heat beneath the ageing Aussie for the remaining 90 seconds. It proved infallible. Referee Jack Hart raised his arm without hesitation and the Empire trophy was back with the Curvis family.

The British title was held by Nottingham's Wally Swift, a cycle assembler at the massive Raleigh plant, and Curvis needed a little luck to beat him. Swift injured a knee and the fight had to be put back a month, allowing Brian to repair the damage from a disastrous training camp in London. At Nottingham Ice Rink on November 21, 1960, he turned on a brilliant display, building a clear lead by halfway. Swift was durable, had a useful left hand and sharp ring intelligence, but in the ninth a right jab followed by a left cross spread him flat on his back. He rose at nine, but the Welshman dropped him with another left before the round was over. The verdict was clear-cut.

Six months later the Midlander had a chance of revenge, at the same venue, but once more Curvis established control in the opening sessions before flooring his man twice in a round. Again Swift survived the full 15 – indeed, 15 and a bit, as neither man heard the bell and their seconds had to dive in and part them. When Mr Hart lifted Brian's hand, some of Wally's more misguided followers threw a few bottles, but neutral observers had no qualms about the verdict.

Brian admires the Lonsdale Belt with promoters Jack Solomons (left) and Syd Wignall

Curvis brushed aside challenges from Mick Leahy, a redhead from Cork, who had taken out British citizenship to become eligible, and Cockney-Italian Tony Mancini, knocking out the first and halting the second on cuts. Curvis suffered similar injuries when his unbeaten record disappeared against ranked American Guy Sumlin at Wembley, but won a rematch and claimed a disqualification win over future world champion Ralph Dupas.

Back on the domestic scene, Bootle gravedigger Tony Smith, the Central Area champion, was floored six times, before an achilles injury sidelined Curvis for eight months. He returned in a non-title clash with British lightweight king Dave Charnley at Wembley, where ringrust hampered him in the early rounds. The 'Dartford Destroyer' floored him in the eighth and Brian had to call upon all his spoiling skills to survive. But he was the better boxer over the piece and it was to the Curvis corner that Mr Hart turned at the bell.

Solomons tried to set up a return, with Curvis's titles at stake, but the Board insisted he defend against Johnny Cooke. With Cliff in his corner for the first time – blood relatives had previously been banned as seconds – Brian showed the Coney Beach fans his full repertoire, winning his second

Curvis faces the mighty Emile Griffith

Lonsdale Belt outright when he forced the crewcut Merseysider to quit at the end of the fifth.

Now, at last, came the big one. Griffith, the 26-year-old from the Virgin Islands, had twice lost the welter crown and regained it – once with tragic consequences, when Benny Paret died following their third encounter. Inevitably, that tragedy was prominent in the pre-fight coverage. Curvis, who had been at ringside for the fatal bout, was as responsible as anyone. "I have a date next week with a killer," he wrote in the *Sunday Mirror*, hardly a comforting thought for his recently acquired bride, Barbara, who refused to attend, despite the champion's gift of a specially crafted hat.

It took £25,000 of Solomons's money to tempt Griffith to Wembley on September 22, 1964. Emile had never faced a southpaw and trainer Gil Clancy took the threat seriously enough to have flown to Wales to watch Curvis against Cooke.

The Welsh fans were in fine voice as the boxers gloved up, but there was little for them to sing about afterwards. Griffith immediately displayed his class with a two-fisted assault which left Brian's face blotched red by the end of the opener. He was being trapped on the ropes and when a left in the sixth jolted Emile into punitive action, a left-right double sent the Welshman down for eight, though the bell curtailed the champion's onslaught.

A body shot floored the challenger in the 10th, but somehow he found the strength to come back in the 11th, and for the first time Griffith was in trouble; this time the champion was the one happy to hear the bell, but the 13th again saw Brian on the floor. From then on, it was a matter of survival until the inevitable raising of Griffith's arm at the close. The champion wept in his triumph, while Brian merely commented, "I lost to a far better man."

Curvis was criticised – by Cliff, among others – for allowing Griffith to take the initiative, but there were other factors involved. Days before the bout, Brian was hospitalized with internal bleeding caused by a medicine ball dropped on his stomach by his brother, who nevertheless insisted the fight should go ahead. When the challenger discovered afterwards that Cliff had bet against him, it shattered their relationship; the pair never spoke to each other again.

Another brother, Ken, took over his training and Brian impressively defeated top men like Mexican Gaspar Ortega and Cubans Isaac Logart and José Stable, with a 12th-round stoppage of London Scot Sammy McSpadden at Sophia Gardens Pavilion retaining his British and Empire titles. But there was also a disputed points defeat in Johannesburg to local hero Willie Ludick and a more conclusive defeat in Paris on April 25, 1966, when he met Jean Josselin, a lathe operator from Besançon, for the vacant European crown. The Frenchman's head-down style inflicted a succession of injuries around Brian's eyes, with the Welshman finding little protection from the referee. Driven around the ring in the 12th and 13th rounds, he retired in his corner.

A stoppage win at Carmarthen over fellow southpaw Des Rea, a Liverpool-based Ulsterman, was intended as a dignified farewell, but it was announced from the ring that Curtis Cokes, who took over after Griffith moved up to middleweight, had agreed to defend against him in Texas. Yet the Board would not recognise it, insisting he defended his own crowns against old rival Cooke. With that troublesome achilles playing up again, a frustrated Curvis relinquished his titles and announced his retirement. It was a decision he later regretted, but the die was cast.

He went on to promote, in partnership with businessman Eddie Richards, dabbled in newspapers and TV, worked for a property group and turned his hand to hotel management. He settled in Middlesbrough and died there, aged 74, after a long battle with leukaemia.

CLIFF CURVIS
(1927–2009)

- **Empire Welterweight Champion 1952**
- **British Welterweight Champion 1952-1953**
- **European Welterweight Challenger 1953**

Boxing in Wales is often a family affair, but surprisingly only one tribe has produced more than one British champion. The Curvises of Swansea – more properly the Nancurvises, although they never used the full Cornish name – were almost obliged to don the leather gloves: after all, their father was little Dai.

Dai Curvis was useful, winning an Army title at bantamweight while serving in India with the South Wales Borderers. Back in civvy street he became a boilerman's assistant in Swansea's dry docks, while advising a whole string of local youngsters wanting to make names for themselves in the ring.

Eldest son Les was a hard-hitting amateur middleweight who died in action at Monte Cassino, building a bridge which still bears the name Nancurvis; the war also ruined the hopes of second son Ken, whose career lost four years to the RAF. But No 3, Cliff, was too young for the call-up. He could do his fighting in the ring at the Premier club, and soon built up quite a reputation. He first tried the sport at eight. At 14 he held a Welsh junior title, at 15 he beat the senior champion, at 16 he was a pro.

The young milkman picked up seven straight wins before the first bump in the road to the top. Frankie Williams, of Birkenhead, was himself unbeaten and a fortnight short of his 21st birthday. Once he began to land his heavier blows, the tiring Swansea boy started to hold;

A young Cliff Curvis

by the seventh round the referee's patience had evaporated and Cliff was disqualified. It was not to be the last time.

The unfortunate ending did nothing to damage Curvis's confidence, and 1946 brought a succession of victories, including revenge over Williams, which took the Welshman to a featherweight eliminator with the famed 'Aldgate Tiger', Al Phillips. In the second round the referee broke them up and warned the Welshman for lying on. "He was still holding my arm when Al caught me with a right to the jaw that sent me staggering across the ring," recalled Cliff, indignantly. Three more rights in succession dropped him to his knees, where he remained throughout the count.

Cliff lands a left on Eddie Thomas

By now Curvis was working out of Swansea Docks, rowing up and down the Bristol Channel, trying to keep track of the shifting mudbanks. The job put muscles on those slender shoulders and he could no longer scale 9st with ease. It was time to try the lightweights. Progress through the new division saw Cliff write the final chapter in the story of Swansea legend Ronnie James, who, weight-weakened, was pulled out after seven rounds. Not that the winner emerged unscathed, being floored as he left the ring by an unexpected punch. It was thrown by Ronnie's wife!

Despite an upset defeat by 20-year-old Peter Fallon, from Birkenhead, on the Freddie Mills-Gus Lesnevich bill at the White City, Curvis destroyed Peckham's Claude Dennington to earn a final eliminator against Scottish champion Harry Hughes at Abergavenny in January, 1949. The 26-year-old boilermaker from Wishaw grabbed his unexpected opportunity with both fists, hustling Curvis out of his elegant style and closing both his eyes before Dai called a halt at the end of the fifth.

Cliff was now a natural welter and the added poundage on his 5ft 10in frame brought an increase in power, but the year ended as it had begun, with two defeats, one the result of a loss of concentration against former Welsh welter ruler Gwyn Williams at Abergavenny, who knocked him out in the fifth. Curvis redeemed himself by taking every round against the veteran former British champion, Ernie Roderick, before returning to Abergavenny for a second crack at Williams, with a British title shot beckoning the winner. This time Gwyn was outpointed; at last Cliff had won an eliminator.

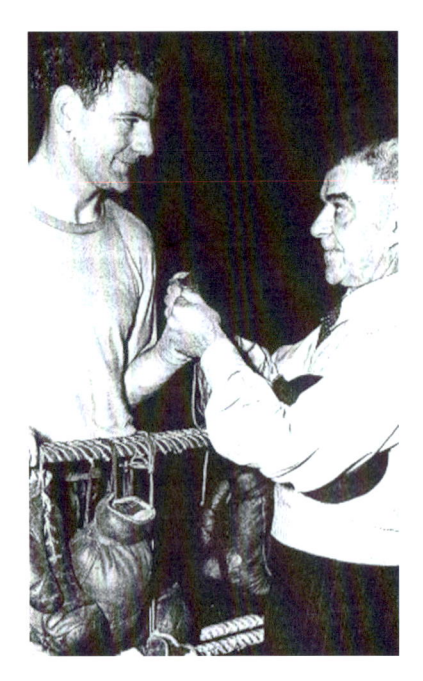

Cliff Curvis is gloved up by father Dai

Before his chance at fellow-countryman Eddie Thomas came disaster on an open-air show at Porthcawl's Coney Beach. Frenchman Charles Humez floored him in the second, and then in the eighth the Swansea man's right eye closed like a trap. There was consternation in the Curvis corner when it was realised they had no ice pack, but an ice cream vendor came to the rescue. A couple of threepenny ones placed where Humez had landed a fourpenny one, and the crisis was resolved. But Charles was still able to use Cliff's "blind" side to advantage in the closing rounds and took a clear verdict.

It was not the best way to go into a title shot, but Curvis, who had prepared in Liverpool, sparring with veteran former featherweight king Nel Tarleton under the supervision of former victim James, put up the best performance of his career before his vociferous hometown fans at St Helen's on September 14, 1950. Many of them would never agree with Jack Hart's decision that Thomas was still champion.

The fight was a disappointment, Mr Hart frequently urging the pair to put more effort in and at one stage threatened to disqualify them both. Thomas, who dislocated his jaw in the fourth and was cut over the right eye in the 10th, initiated what action there was, while Curvis had his best moments with counters. Cliff took a knee in the sixth, complaining of a low blow, but the referee blamed the local for jumping as the punch was thrown.

It was back to the drawing-board. After a six-month break, Curvis resumed his climb towards a title shot. Once more, though, the Welshman's dreams were to be frustrated. The final eliminator, at Liverpool Stadium, brought him up against 25-year-old Wally Thom, like himself a southpaw, and a former amateur star – he won the Welsh ABA title while stationed here in the Army – who had won 21 on the trot as a pro. He also came from that town that figured so insistently in Cliff's story: Birkenhead.

It was nip and tuck, with both men concentrating on the body, and there was little to choose between them when, in the ninth round, a hard left to the stomach buckled Curvis at the knees. When he recovered, he forced Wally to the ropes and earned a warning for butting. Thom seemed in some discomfort and before referee Peter Muir could signal them to box on, Cliff crashed home a left to the head. Mr Muir immediately disqualified him.

By the end of the year, Thom had unseated Eddie Thomas and Curvis was given a straight shot at the new holder. The first British title fight between two southpaws took place on July 24, 1952, at Liverpool Stadium, already regarded as the 'Graveyard of Champions'.

Despite their earlier result, Curvis was a firm favourite because of his longer experience, and the betting boys were as shrewd as ever. A packed house watched a Thom below his best, unable to cope with Cliff's left hook, and the first round saw Wally on the floor twice. The die was cast, although it was a solid right from the local man which sparked the decisive exchanges in the ninth: Curvis responded by pushing Wally to the ropes and landing

Curvis flattens Wally Thom

a perfect left hook to the chin. Thom rose groggily at six, only to stagger into a barrage which left him reeling, with his head hanging through the ropes, before slipping to the deck again. He clambered up at two, but Cliff knew it was all over. One left hook to the stomach finished it, referee Hart reaching 10 as the dethroned champion lurched to his feet.

With the British crown had come that of the Empire, and Cliff was tempted to South Africa – unusually for the time, he flew – to defend against Gerald Dreyer, a 23-year-old former Olympic champion from Pretoria who had just collected 11 consecutive wins in North America. A 10,000 crowd at the Rand Stadium in Johannesburg, on December 8, 1952, cheered their man home, but only after a deal of controversy. The champion had been frequently warned for hitting on the break, then still legal in Britain, but managed to establish a points lead over the first five rounds. Then came the incident that turned the fight. Cliff landed a peach of a left uppercut: the South African slumped to the canvas and the referee began to count.

"In those days in Britain we used to stand behind the ref, in the middle of the ring, while he counted," explained Cliff. "Out there you had to go to a neutral corner. So he suddenly broke off, took me to a corner, lectured me for a couple of seconds and then started counting again from one." Dreyer waited until nine before rising, still shaky, but able to survive till the bell. Not only had the challenger been down for a good 16 seconds, but Cliff's left hand had suffered as much damage as Dreyer's chin and was virtually useless from then on. The title duly changed hands.

Cliff's other venture into foreign parts produced similar disillusion. On March 22, 1953, he crossed swords with Frenchman Gilbert Lavoine at the Mutualité in Paris for the European belt vacated by old rival Humez. Apart from the second round, when that trademark Curvis left hook put Lavoine down for four, it was a sad affair, with both warned repeatedly for holding. Eventually, in the 10th, Belgian ref Gilbert de Munter disqualified Curvis to the cheers of a crowd as relieved to see the end of the affair as they were pleased to welcome a French victory. The loser's purse was at first withheld, although later restored in full, and the European Boxing Union suspended Mr de Munter for his "lack of authority" during the contest.

The last hurrah as Cliff (right) tangles with Gilbert Lavoine

It was a poor way to end a glittering career. For Curvis, just 25, but newly married, never boxed again, handing in his British title in protest at the pittance he was offered to defend it by the recently knighted Porthcawl fairground operator, Sir Leslie Joseph. "After paying tax and my training expenses I'd have had less than £400," he said. "Not much, when you consider I'd been getting £1,000 a fight at 18."

Cliff went into the credit business and then land development, before taking over the licence of a Swansea pub for a few years. But he was never far from the sport that brought him fame. He managed brother Brian to the very titles he had held himself and also worked with British lightweight champion Maurice Cullen and heavyweight king Neville Meade.

He spent nearly 40 years in various roles with the Welsh Area Council and the Board of Control, finally retiring as Administrative Steward in 1998, a decade before his death at 81.

KEN CURVIS
(1922–1980)

🥊 Welsh Welterweight Challenger 1950

The second son of legendary Swansea trainer Dai Curvis was one of a lost generation. Just as he was setting out on a ring career, he received the call to take part in a bigger fight. And by the time he came back from four years' war service in the RAF, his prime was behind him.

Ken had around 20 amateur contests before his father deemed him ready to get paid for his punches, but his debut was somewhat unexpected. He was called up as a substitute to face fellow-townsman Billy Hayes at the Mannesmann Hall and found himself on the wrong end of a six-round decision.

A rematch was quickly arranged, but this time Hayes pulled out and Curvis claimed his first victory at the expense of Maesteg's Vivian Martin. And then the official papers landed on the doormat, taking him away from little Dai's gym until peace returned. Life as a PTI in the RAF had its moments – as a member of the boxing team, he was even provided with servants – and he won the All-India title to repay their generosity, but it was 1947 before he could resume his pro career.

Ken soon built a winning streak, including success over the border, before a setback when he had to retire with a badly gashed lip against Benny Price at Pontardawe, ironically the same injury that had forced the Cross Hands man out of his Welsh title clash with Oxford-based Gwyn Williams three years earlier.

A draw with highly touted southpaw Allan Wilkins, from Ystradgynlais, underlined Curvis's quality and it was further recognised when he was matched with Rhondda boy Les Vaughan at Abergavenny in an eliminator for the Welsh welter title. Ken cut his man and floored him three times

Ken Curvis

on the way to the 10-round decision on a show topped by Eddie Thomas, who went on to claim the crown by dethroning Williams three months later.

With Eddie expected to relinquish the Welsh honour if he became British champion, Ken was paired with the exiled Williams, who had just knocked out brother Cliff. Thomas duly kept his side of the bargain and moved on to bigger things, but Williams opted for a rematch with the younger Curvis to gain the right to oppose the Merthyr man. Cliff gained revenge and brother Ken was given a straight shot at the vacant Welsh throne, with old foe Wilkins in the opposite corner.

They met on June 21, 1950, at Coney Beach, Porthcawl, down the card on the first of promoter Leslie Joseph's summer shows. While Cliff emerged a winner on the night, his older sibling found life a lot harder.

A believer in the old saying that a right hook is the answer to a lefty, Ken kept throwing it, but Wilkins seemed impervious, while scoring frequently enough with his own jabs to bring a trickle of scarlet from the Swansea man's left eyebrow as early as the first round.

The third saw Curvis land one of those right swings with sufficient force to drop Allan for a count of six, but Ken became a bit wild in his efforts to finish matters, prompting a series of warnings as he strayed near the borderline. By the fifth, he was bleeding from the mouth as well as the eye, and looked to be tiring. When another right to the body landed low in the sixth, the referee had seen enough, ordering Curvis to his corner as Wilkins celebrated his new status.

That was that for Ken the boxer. He trained Brian for his last two years in the ring, but once kid brother, too, had retired, it spelt the end of his involvement with the sport as he focussed on earning a living and raising five children with wife Beryl.

GIPSY DANIELS
(1903–1967)

- **British Light-Heavyweight Champion 1927**
- **Welsh Light-Heavyweight Champion 1927–30**

The life of one of Wales's most colourful characters is a whirlpool of fact and fantasy. The most obvious example of the myth is his nom de guerre: the young West Walian had no Romany blood, even if his swarthy complexion might hint that. But somehow other fictions grew around him.

Respected ring historians insisted that he was actually a Danny Thomas, from Newport, while early record books claimed he was born in 1902. It is all the more surprising, given that he came from a well-known family. His father, David John Daniel, a journeyman plasterer, was a Llanelli forward who had won eight caps for Wales in the 1890s, and Billy, one of 13 children, was born in their home on the town's Swansea Road. As for his birth, it needed a letter to *Boxing News* from his brother-in-law to point out that it was a year later than listed.

Either way, in an era when many 13-year-olds were already being paid for their punches, the Llanelli youngster did not enter the fray until his late teens. Usually dubbed simply "Young Daniel", but occasionally as Billy Daniels – note the arrival of the superfluous 's' – he campaigned around the valleys, where his exploits soon caused a bit of a stir, but it was a call from one of Britain's most controversial politicians that was to broaden his horizons.

Horatio Bottomley, a Liberal MP raised in an East End orphanage, owned a patriotic magazine, *John Bull*, and decided it should sponsor a selection of prospects in a bid to

Gipsy Daniels

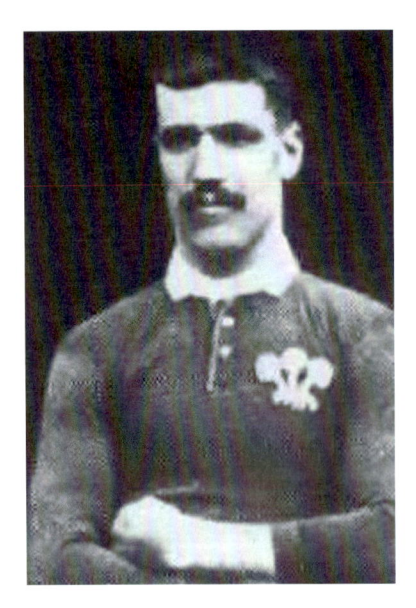

David John Daniel, Billy's old man

restore British boxing's "former glory". Youngsters from all over the country were brought together in the Kent resort of Herne Bay.

After the applicants were whittled down by a series of try-outs, those remaining included several Welshmen, one of them Daniels. The best were eventually deemed ready to be launched on London fight society in a big show at the Albert Hall, but Billy was one of only two to win. The scheme soon collapsed, like many of Bottomley's ideas. The MP, ironically the founder of the *Financial Times*, was twice declared bankrupt and eventually jailed for fraud.

At least the good food available to 'John Bull's Boys' saw Daniels, a welter on arrival, develop into a middleweight. He even entered an open heavyweight competition at the Blackfriars Ring, actually winning his first bout. He made sufficient impact to be invited back for a similar tournament in his own division. Six weeks and five contests later the Welshman was declared the winner, although some thought him lucky and he was booed throughout. It was an experience with which he was to become all too familiar.

The matchmaker at the Ring, Dan Sullivan, took over his management, resulting in regular appearances at the central London venue. But when Billy began to get itchy feet – perhaps his nickname was having an influence – and venture into the wider world he had to look after himself.

Mind you, when he crossed the Atlantic in 1922, he was taken in hand by one of the sport's legends. Liverpool-born James J. Johnston had emigrated to New York at the age of 12, boxing for a while before devoting himself to the business side to such effect that writer Damon Runyon dubbed him 'The Boy Bandit of Broadway'. And one of Johnston's strong points was publicity.

In the "Roaring Twenties", anything went when it came to grabbing headlines. So, once the promoter heard the newcomer's name, he was not about to miss the opportunity. He fitted him out with big brass earrings, a yellow silk bandanna, loose velvet trousers and an embroidered coat. Thus clad, the Welshman was introduced to the local press as a Romany prince.

The new image created quite a stir in the Big Apple, but also back home in Llanelli, prompting his father to write an angry letter, threatening to disown his errant son. After five successful months in the US, Billy headed for home to face parental wrath and a points defeat by Welsh middleweight champion Frank Moody at Newport. The pair would meet again.

Now campaigning among the light-heavyweights, Daniels won a lot more than he lost, although his lack of power meant he was usually forced to rely on the officials' judgment. It was April 11, 1927, almost four years after their first meeting, that he came face to face once more with Moody. Although staged at the Ring, it was recognised as for the vacant Welsh title.

Moody had recently returned from his own, longer sojourn in the States, and had just won the British middle crown. But with potential rivals tied up elsewhere, the Pontypridd man stepped up in weight to face his former victim.

Daniels was already booked for a shot at British and Empire boss Tom Berry a fortnight later, but that plan almost came unstuck. Moody seemed in control from the first bell. Indeed, so one-sided was the contest that, as the pair emerged for the final session, Frank heard one ringside bookie announcing that a Moody victory was 33-1 on. He went through the motions until the conclusion – and then watched in amazement as referee Sam Russell raised Daniels's arm.

Gipsy as the Yanks saw him

Berry, a Londoner who had learned to box while a prisoner-of-war, had won the vacant British championship at the official age of 35; given that he staged a celebration party which included several grandchildren, it is probable that he was well into his forties. Two years later 'Old Tom' added the Empire crown and on April 25, 1927, put both on the line against Daniels at the Holland Park roller skating rink in Kensington. There was little excitement, but the battle was tight enough to hold the interest. Berry tried to increase the pace in the last five rounds, but Billy's youth and speed proved enough to earn the nod.

Gipsy was an unhappy champion, however. Just six months into his reign, he handed back his Lonsdale Belt in a gesture of rebellion that was a significant nail in the coffin of the once all-powerful NSC. He pointed out that the Club's £500 purse for a defence, with the winner taking £300, left just £200 for the loser; given he was expected to find a sidestake of £100, with training expenses accounting for a further £100, defeat would mean

Max Schmeling - Gipsy beat him in a round before Joe Louis did

going home with nothing. He asked the Club for £250 to cover such an outcome, but they offered £100. Not enough, said Daniels, who began to seek better paydays on the Continent.

His first port of call was Berlin, where he took on a young hopeful named Max Schmeling, already European light-heavy champion. After 10 rounds, the 'Black Uhlan' emerged a points winner. But when they met again in Frankfurt on February 25, 1928, there was a very different outcome.

Schmeling was on a 22-fight winning streak. The European belt was not at stake against Daniels – once more it was over 10 rounds and both were well over the weight – but the shock was seismic. Max, still just 22 and full of youthful certainty, raced from his corner in all-out attack. Daniels – a supposed non-puncher, remember – caught him with a straight right to the jaw. The German crumpled and, amid stunned silence, was counted out.

Yet, barely two years later, Schmeling was world heavyweight champion. There had been suggestions of a third meeting, but when the Welshman arrived in Berlin to talk terms he discovered that Max had sailed for New York that morning. His conqueror was left to travel around Europe, with limited success. In 1929 Daniels fought seven times, including scraps in Berlin, Paris and Turin, and came second on each occasion.

Billy boxed on in decent class, earning regularly, but without ever reaching the heights. He had a rubber match with old rival Moody, at the White City dog track in Cardiff's Sloper Road, where an August Bank Holiday crowd of 12,000 saw Frank defy the calendar to capture the Welsh title, outscoring the weight-drained Llanelli man.

There were a couple of hard fights in Germany with Walter Neusel, both lost on points, while his occasional triumphs included two wins (and a draw) against Jack London and another two wins (and a loss) against Reggie Meen. Both went on to wear the British heavyweight crown.

Based in Derby in later years, under the management of a local hotelier, Billy toured with a fairground booth and saw off a series of journeymen before departing the scene in 1938. Yet he still had one contribution to make: a Bournemouth teenager named Freddie Mills joined the booth and the Welsh veteran became his mentor, teaching him all the tricks of the trade.

Well, most of them. After their "fights", each would go around the crowd collecting "nobbings".

Gipsy in 1966 with Harry Morris, mayor of Llanelli

When it came to sharing the spoils, Freddie was always surprised to find that Billy only had coppers to add to the pot, whereas he himself had a fair few silver coins each time. It was only when he accidentally donned his partner's dressing-gown that he discovered a hoard of shillings and sixpences in the left-hand pocket; Billy had dispensed his pennies and ha'pennies from the right. It was another of life's lessons learned.

While Mills would go on to rule the planet's light-heavyweights, Daniels soon drifted away from the sport. He moved to Plymouth to work in the naval dockyard, living there until his death at the age of 64.

Billy may not be one of our greatest ringmen, but he was certainly a larger-than-life figure who deserved the civic reception he was given when he made a trip home to Llanelli in 1966. And he remains the only Welshman ever to knock out a world heavyweight champion.

GLYNNE DAVIES
(1943–   )

🥊 Welsh Bantamweight Champion 1979–80

"Three tries for a Welshman", or so the old saying goes. And sometimes it rings true. It certainly proved correct for the Llanelli southpaw. Twice he contested the Welsh bantam title, twice he failed. But the third attempt saw him capture the national belt – more than 17 years after his pro debut!

Ewart Glynne Davies, the only boxer of six sons, was a useful amateur, winning a Welsh ABA championship. But he was passed over for Commonwealth Games selection and signed up with the illustrious Eddie Thomas, beginning with a two-round stoppage of fellow-teenager Billy Thomas, using his purse to buy bikes for two of his brothers.

A week later Glynne (mis-spelt Glyn throughout his career) discovered the other side of the coin in an up-and-downer with Halifax newcomer Tommy Atkins. Each had been down twice when the Yorkshireman landed a right to the jaw which felled Davies for the full count. But it had little effect on Glynne's confidence as he proceeded to win his next six, four of them via stoppage.

The young labourer overcame decent rivals such as Southern Area champion Don Weller and one-time British flyweight challenger Tony Barlow, but twice fell short against former eight-stone champion Jackie Brown. A draw in South Africa and a knockout triumph in Sweden boosted his reputation and his bank balance before he was matched with a young Cardiffian for the vacant Welsh bantam throne.

Steve Curtis, though an amateur star, had found the transition to the paid ranks difficult, with a loss and a draw scarring his first four bouts. Yet he was picked to face Davies, who could point to 42 fights over seven years, at Sophia Gardens Pavilion on July 2, 1969. But youth triumphed over experience as the 20-year-old local, defying predictions that he would fade in the later rounds, came back from an early deficit. He took over after the sixth, hurting Glynne with several big rights, to take the referee's verdict by a two-round margin.

Davies found little solace in a trip to Italy, where he was halted in three by fellow-southpaw Franco Zurlo, who won the European bantam crown in his next outing. But he was given a return against Curtis, this time at the National Sporting Club's home in London's West End. Alas, Glynne came in two pounds overweight and then allowed the skilful champion to outbox him and collect Jim Brimmell's decision.

Things went from bad to worse. The Llanelli man was stopped in his next three contests, by reigning British fly boss John McCluskey, in Barcelona by Ghanaian-born future European king Bob Allotey and by unbeaten Paddy Maguire, later to rule Britain's bantams.

Yet he had influential backing on home ground and when Curtis surprisingly retired, still short of his 21st birthday, Glynne was paired with Tonyrefail's Colin Miles, who had succeeded to his throne. They came together at Afan Lido on October 19, 1970, and the challenger's chances were soon hampered by damage to his left hand. Miles was already on top, however, and Davies – dropped by a stiff right in the seventh – offered no excuses when the third man raised the Rhondda man's arm.

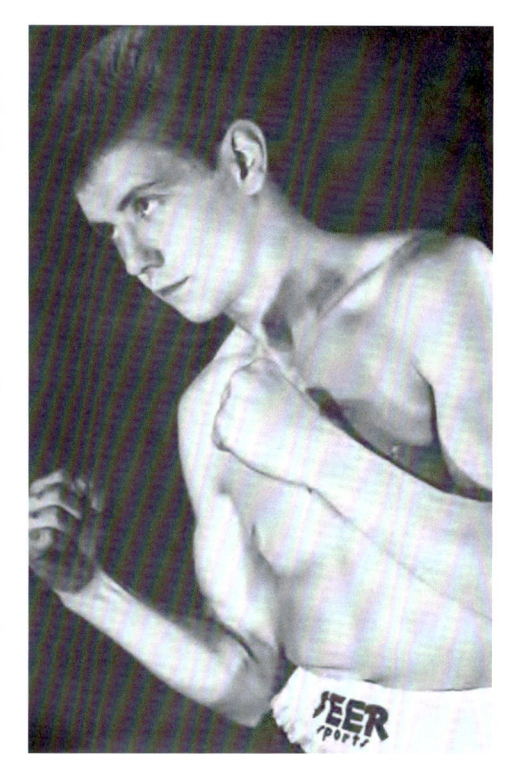

Glynne Davies

Glynne was also suffering regularly from cuts and hinted at retirement if he bled again in an eight-rounder with Liverpudlian Billy Hardacre at the Afan Lido. In the event he was gashed over both eyes and lost a points decision. It was enough: he switched to the safe side of the ropes to manage heavyweight ace Neville Meade. But the itch had to be scratched and four years later he returned to the ring.

Unbeaten prospect Jeff Pritchard was hardly the easiest first opponent to choose and the New Tredegar boy duly took the verdict, though Glynne's performance convinced him there was life in the old dog yet. But after being cut and halted next time out he took another lengthy break.

Then, a week before his 36th birthday, he was back, wowing the dinner-suited audience at the National Sporting Club. This time he kept active and seven months later reached the pinnacle he must have long given up hope of achieving. Promoter Heddwyn Taylor put him in with awkward Pip Coleman for the vacant Welsh bantam title on October 4, 1979, at Ebbw Vale Leisure Centre.

It was a messy affair – almost a given where the unorthodox Coleman was involved – but Davies employed his counter-punching skills to ward off the all-action miner from Neath. The inevitable close-quarter encounters had their equally inevitable outcome and Pip suffered a gash along the left eyebrow. At the end of the seventh, referee Adrian Morgan considered the wound too bad for Coleman to continue, not an opinion shared by the diminutive victim. But Glynne had finally claimed the national honour to go with that won as an amateur more than 17 years earlier.

It was the last time he enjoyed victory. After four straight defeats – including a retirement loss in a non-title clash with British titleholder Johnny Owen – Davies faced Coleman again at Swansea's Top Rank Suite on October 1, 1980, three days short of a year into Glynne's reign. Pip's methods had not changed. He just kept walking in, whirling his fists in the general direction of his opponent, and enjoying a fair amount of success against someone who lacked the mobility of his early years. It was no shock when Mr Morgan decided that the belt should change hands.

The ex-champion carried on for a couple of months, but when Sussex prospect Paul Huggins sparked him in 87 seconds, that was that. Davies turned back to management, running a gym outside Llanelli's railway station, and staying in good nick by running marathons.

SHON DAVIES
(1986–   )

🥊 Welsh Light-Heavyweight Champion 2008–11

It was not a good omen. The teenage flanker wanted to make a farewell appearance for Penygroes RFC before he set out on a new career as a professional boxer. With a date already set for his debut contest, he told the club he would come on for the last 10 minutes as a replacement. But, seconds after taking the field, he dislocated a shoulder.

Never before injured on the rugby pitch, Shon Aled Davies was forced to postpone his entry into the paid ring. And when the Llanelli youngster finally climbed through the ropes in Dagenham to face unbeaten Richard Horton he found himself on the canvas before the bell's echoes had died away. But Davies clambered up to stop the Essex man midway through the opener.

It was some introduction for the 19-year-old steelworker from Gorslas, whose career at Towy ABC had coincided with the split in Welsh amateur circles. Davies, who first gloved up at the age of nine, under the supervision of father Paul, won national schoolboy championships on both sides of the divide, but his one attempt at the senior ABAs came a cropper against future pro Tobias Webb.

With Hywel Davies – universally known as 'Cass' – in the manager's seat, Shon followed the win over Horton with an even quicker demolition job on the much heavier Nicki Taylor, as he picked up four straight successes. A one-point defeat by Midlander Tyrone Wright on his own territory meant little, even if Davies's next loss, in three rounds to big-hitting Commonwealth Games gold medallist Kenny Anderson, perhaps indicated the Carmarthen-born youngster's position in the wider scheme of things.

Shon Davies

Shon and 'Cass' with the Welsh belt

But he had beaten all three Welsh opponents he had faced and the area council agreed he should meet Cardiffian Wayne Brooks for their vacant light-heavyweight crown. Brooks had also lost his previous contest in three rounds, at the heavy hands of future world title challenger Tony Bellew, so the pair were in the same boat as far as dented confidence was concerned, although Wayne could point to an amateur decision over the West Walian, while Davies was punching hard enough to snap a rib of sparmate Adam Wilcox.

They came together at the Afan Lido on March 30, 2008, for the first Welsh title clash at the weight for a quarter of a century, and it lived up to its billing – even if promoter Nick Hodges discovered to his cost that paying punters were loath to leave their Sunday dinner tables.

Most of those who did turn up were backing Brooks, who basked in their welcome. Davies, in contrast, slipped into the arena almost unnoticed. Yet within a minute of the first bell, Wayne was on his back, courtesy of a left hook from Shon, and the clan from the capital fell silent.

Brooks was on the retreat for much of the next two sessions, although his greater variety of punch was occasionally obvious, but a switch to southpaw at the start of the fourth indicated a swing in fortunes. The new stance enabled Wayne to sink his right into Davies's body, a tactic which soon paid off as the West Walian began to tire. By the end of the sixth Shon was a sad figure on his stool, coughing up phlegm and clutching his painful side. It took all his manager's oratorical skills to convince him that he should emerge for the seventh.

But a fight can turn in an instant. Brooks stepped back from a close-quarter exchange with blood pouring from a gash over his right eye; Davies, with renewed energy, stormed in two-fisted and, after a further minute or so, referee Wynford Jones led the Cardiff man back to his corner, took a close look at the wound, and waved his arms. Shon was the new champion.

But it did not signify a step into the big time. There was a shot at the newly introduced Prizefighter event, which saw Davies ousted in his first bout by former Olympian Courtney Fry. There were two bids in two months for the largely decorative International Masters belt, Sheffielder Billy Boyle outpointing Shon before former British and Commonwealth king Tony Oakey halted him in three.

More than three years had passed since the Brooks victory when Davies was finally invited to defend his national supremacy, with Talywain's Jeff Evans, whose only loss had come in a Prizefighter tournament at super-middleweight, in the other corner at the Newport Centre on May 7, 2011.

Davies stormed out quickly, as if hoping to overwhelm the comparatively inexperienced challenger. But, with the calming influence of former pro Gary Lockett in his corner, Evans gradually took control. By the sixth, Shon was breathing hard and a left beneath the ribs dropped him to one knee in the closing seconds. There was no time for 'Jeffro' to follow up, but no matter: the Davies corner retired their man.

Since then it has been back to the rugby field and his old team-mates at Penygroes, where he is now captain. Boxing is a thing of the past – or is it?

ROBERT DICKIE
(1964–2010)

- British Featherweight Champion 1986–88
- British Super-Featherweight Champion 1991
- WBC International Featherweight Champion 1988
- Scottish Featherweight Champion 1985

The man from Cross Hands was always a bit of a pioneer. He was the first Welsh-speaker to win a Scottish title. He was the first Briton to win one of the second-tier straps that now infest the sport like a plague. And he was one of the few Welshmen to have worn a Lonsdale Belt at two weights. That alone marks him out as someone special.

Robert Glyndŵr Dickie was born in Carmarthen, one of the eight children of a Scottish lorry driver, and his ambition was obvious from the start. When his class at Maes-yr-Yrfa were asked to draw pictures of what they wanted to be when they grew up, the 11-year-old Robert handed in a sketch of himself in the ring, with the caption 'Champion Boxer'.

His first steps in that direction came at Blaenau ABC, where North Walian John Davies was in charge, winning a Welsh ABA championship before turning pro with Swansea promoter Colin Breen, to be trained by Jimmy Bromfield, whose scorn for the new recruit's Cross Hands home gave birth to a nickname. "It's like Chickasaw County where you come from," Bromfield told him. Dickie loved it, promptly labelling himself 'The Chickasaw County Kid'.

Dickie had to travel for his first three fights, including a trip to Aberdeen, where mention

Robert Dickie

of his Scottish parentage alerted the authorities. After four straight wins, he was held to a draw in Glasgow by Edinburgh prospect Danny Flynn. The Gilmour family, who ran St Andrew's Sporting Club, promptly invited Robert back for a rematch for the Scottish bantamweight crown.

But the Welshman was having problems at the weight and Flynn stopped him in the fifth. It was the signal for a move up to feather, where he was soon called upon for a shot at another vacant Scottish title. In the other corner, ringwise Glaswegian John Sharkey, who had been disqualified for butting Dickie three months earlier.

When they came together on February 25, 1985, again under the St Andrew's Club banner, Sharkey had little opportunity for illicit headwork. Two solid right hands dropped John twice in the second session; on the second occasion he lay beneath the bottom rope as referee Billy Rafferty tolled the count. Only afterwards – and this was his second title fight, remember – did the Scottish Area Council abruptly decide that Robert was not eligible after all, promptly stripping him.

Not that there was much sleep lost, with Dickie moving closer to British honours. A left-right combination destroyed the unbeaten record of Londoner Mark Reefer in just 78 seconds, before he travelled to South Africa, floored local hero Frank Khonkhobe three times and was "rewarded" with a draw.

Six months later, on April 9, 1986, Robert took on Hartlepool's John Feeney in the opulent surroundings of the Albert Hall for the British feather strap vacated by Barry McGuigan. Feeney was a nine-year pro whose 44 contests had seen two spells as bantam king; Dickie, six years

Dickie (right) takes on John Feeney

younger at 21, was very much second favourite. But the pair put on a titanic tussle before the underdog was proclaimed the new champion by a mere half-point. Referee Larry O'Connell's decision saw the stunned Feeney sag against the ropes in disappointment, while manager Dennie Mancini, who had objected when the official was given the job, was full of righteous indignation.

At the end of the day, it was a close contest which was always destined to provoke outrage in the backers of the man on the short end. Dickie recovered from a slow start to land some firm rights to the head, while Feeney responded to the body, not always fairly. The seventh saw the Tees-sider sent reeling into a corner post after shipping Robert's dangerous right, but he battled back to bring blood from the Welshman's nose, before again being shaken by three successive rights in the 10th. After a toe-to-toe final session, it was anyone's fight; for the man who counted, it was Dickie's.

The Feeney camp demanded an immediate rematch, but the Board approved the new champion's plan for an all-Welsh defence at Ebbw Vale Leisure Centre against former holder Steve 'Sammy' Sims. The Newport man was on the downslope of an excellent career; Dickie was heading upwards. Sims was tight at the weight, but began on the offensive, boring in behind his trademark peekaboo guard. Robert soon found the key, launching regular uppercuts before switching his attention to the body. And it was a left beneath the challenger's ribs two seconds from the end of the fifth which closed the show, referee John Coyle counting through the bell as Steve, on all fours, struggled to regain his breath.

Next up was Feeney, who headed for Ebbw Vale with a sense of injustice. Another full house saw the visitor's hopes dented by an opening round in which Dickie dropped him twice. But an equally explosive second saw Robert wobbled, although he was never to be seriously troubled thereafter. This time there were no arguments; indeed, Feeney raised Dickie's arm even before referee Roland Dakin could do so. Robert had won a Lonsdale Belt outright in 203 days, just one day faster than previous record-holder Pat Cowdell.

The youngster seemed on the verge of great things. But fate had other ideas: a Sunday-afternoon car crash left him with a broken back and his career in jeopardy. He spent six weeks in hospital and another five in a plaster cast, but, happily, made a full recovery, though it was a year before he was back in action. The Board allowed him two rust-removing outings, but when a hand injury forced Robert out of a defence against former stablemate Peter Harris, their patience ran out and they stripped him of the title.

Dickie was nominated to face Belgian Jean-Marc Renard for the vacant European crown, but was already booked for a scrap up at super-feather for the WBC's new International belt, for boxers between 11 and 20 in its rankings. On March 29, 1988, on a dinner show in Stoke, Dickie halted Indonesian holder Hengky Gun in five rounds. It was an inch-long gash over the left eyelid which brought the end, but the preceding action had been totally one-sided, Gun was out of ammunition and there were no complaints at the stoppage.

Five months later Dickie was back in Stoke to defend his new belt against Kamel Bou-Ali, a 30-year-old Italian-based Tunisian, who had already challenged for the WBA title. And the rough, tough African's old head won him the fight, if not for any innate wisdom; tolerated by lenient referee Armand Krief, Bou-Ali bored in from the start and the Welshman's face soon began to mark up. A fifth-round butt split the champion's left eyebrow in horrendous fashion – it needed 12 stitches – and it was over in the sixth.

A disillusioned Dickie vanished from the gym, playing a little rugby for Cefneithin and indulging in a few pints. An angry Breen pulled him out of a mandated challenge to new British champion Floyd Havard, insisting that he would not renew the boxer's contract when it expired. Robert finally rang him to explain that he had needed a break after 13 years; the pair made up and agreed a new three-year deal. But a week before his ring return Dickie changed his mind, announcing his retirement.

There was a two-bout comeback, then another lengthy disappearing act underlined his waning interest. But when he returned to break the jaw of Canadian champion Barrington Francis, it opened the door for another title shot. At the Welsh National Sports Centre on March 5, 1991, Dickie took on the British super-feather king, Kevin Pritchard, a Liverpudlian with a spotty record who had knocked out Midlander Hugh Forde to claim the throne.

That one-punch finish and the feeling of a belt

Robert Dickie on the heavy bag

around his waist clearly boosted Pritchard's confidence and he totally dominated the first two rounds, with Dickie lucky to make it through. Having survived the initial onslaught, Robert gradually took over as the holder tired. Come the eighth, a series of rights to the body completed his task: down three times, Kevin was unable to beat referee Roy Francis's count. Pritchard had three cracked ribs; Dickie was a two-weight champion.

A swift defence was arranged at Stockport Town Hall against Sugar Gibiliru, another Scouse journeyman whose stats had suddenly improved. A below-par Dickie tired early and, cut above and below the right eye, was being beaten up when referee John Coyle stepped between them in the ninth. In effect, it marked the end of Robert's career.

There was a brief reappearance two and a half years later, but a cut-eye defeat by Hereford's Phil Found convinced Dickie to call it a day. He was not to enjoy retirement for long. At just 46, the 'Chickasaw County Kid' died from a heart attack. A charitable trust has been set up in his memory.

DAVE GEORGE
(1959–)

🥊 British Flyweight Challenger 1982

It was unusual, to say the least, to have a British championship bout as the curtain-raiser to a big show. Perhaps the fact that it involved two Welshmen, but was taking place at Wembley Arena, might explain the apparent disrespect.

Fans back in Wales wondered what they had done to miss out on the clash for the flyweight throne vacated by Charlie Magri. Kelvin Smart and Swansea's Dave George had each lost only once, both in foreign fields, although both defeats had come in their previous outings. The Llanbradach man had been outpointed by Olympic medallist Enrique Rodríguez Cal in a European final eliminator in Spain, while George had dropped a decision in Geneva to unbeaten Frenchman Antoine Montero, later a three-time world title challenger.

Dave had earned his chance with a 98-second demolition job on former British ABA champion Gary Nickels in a final eliminator at Ebbw Vale. The Paddington prospect had been highly favoured, especially as George had been floored on his way to

Dave George (right) and brother Don

victory over Ulster journeyman Neil McLaughlin two fights earlier. But on a card which saw big brother Don become Welsh featherweight champion, Dave dropped Nickels with a left to the chin before pinning him in a neutral corner until referee Jim Brimmell leapt between them.

Promoter Heddwyn Taylor vowed to bring the George-Smart decider to Wales, but Kelvin was managed by Mickey Duff, who had featured him regularly on his big London shows, and the veteran wheeler-dealer was not to be denied. At least supporters travelling from Swansea on September 14, 1982, had other incentives to make the long journey, with Colin and Peter Jones both in action. The brothers duly won, but Dave found life a lot more painful.

Former world champion Ken Buchanan had visited Winch Wen to help out, staying with the family, but it made little difference. From the opening bell, it was Kelvin moving forward, with George trying to keep him at bay with his left. But the West Walian lacked the power for that tactic to succeed and he began to ship hooks to the body as Smart closed the gap between them. By the fourth he was clearly in difficulty and slipped to the canvas in the fifth, when Smart was ticked off for throwing a punch before his foe could rise.

Come the sixth and the writing was well and truly on the wall. Two left hooks, one up top and the other down below, forced Dave to back away. Smart leapt after him, driving him to the ropes and whipping in another left to the body. George sagged to the floor and never looked like beating referee Sid Nathan's count.

Dave was only 22 and his dreams were already shattered. Hopes had been so high when he swept through the junior ranks under the tuition of father Eric, himself a champion in the Army. He collected a cupboardful of trophies, before winning the Welsh ABA flyweight title in his first senior bout. His second, in the British semi-final, was against future WBC king Magri, so it was no surprise when he was stopped in the opener.

George added two more Welsh championships at bantam and competed in both European and Commonwealth tournaments, losing each time to one of the medallists. In 1979 he turned pro with Reading-based Bev Walker, with Brighton-based Irishman Paddy Byrne eventually taking over. It was not until the Nickels eliminator that Dave made his first paid appearance in Wales.

It was a similar story when he returned to the ring after the Smart setback. His next eight fights included two in Belfast and another two in Glasgow, but nothing in the land of his fathers.

There was a bid to break into the British bantamweight title race with an eliminator against former Olympian Ray Gilbody on February 20, 1984, at the National Sporting Club, but the unbeaten Merseysider floored him three times before the diminutive Nathan, the man who had counted him out against Smart, came to the rescue midway through the second round.

Gilbody went on to dethrone British boss John Feeney; George, after another stoppage at the hands of future world champion Dave McAuley, vanished from the scene for three years.

When he resumed in 1987, it was with former heavyweight Ron Gray, so his activity centred on the Midlands, with wins and losses against decent opposition, before he went on a little run of four straight victories, including a decision over Pembrokeshire traveller Renny Edwards at the Patti Pavilion in his only pro bout in his home city.

Dave flattens Gary Nickels

But two points defeats – against ex-amateur ace Peter English and, in France, Jean-Pierre Dibateza – were followed by a stoppage loss in Doncaster at the hands of local prospect Peter Gabbitus and Dave decided, after almost exactly a decade as pro, to call it a day.

Outside the ropes, the former fitter and turner became a horticulturist with B&Q, for whom he has worked for more than 30 years. But boxing was consigned to history.

DON GEORGE
(1957–   )

🥊 Welsh Featherweight Champion 1981–83

Azumah Nelson was perhaps the greatest boxer to emerge from Africa, with 13 almost unbroken years as world champion. Fans will remember the brave attempts by Pat Cowdell and Jim McDonnell to knock him off his throne: Cowdell was halted in the first at featherweight, while 'Jimmy Mac' lasted until the 12th at super-feather.

But there was a third Briton who traded punches with 'The Professor'. And Don George did so in the Ghanaian's back yard.

The oldest of four fighting brothers from Winch Wen – Dave and Eric both boxed pro, while Terry was a schoolboy champion – Don first made his name in the colours of Swansea Docks ABC, with a hat-trick of Welsh schoolboy titles matched by another three at junior level. He stepped up to the seniors and claimed three more successes in the Welsh ABAs, although he lost each time in the British semi-finals – once to that man Cowdell.

Don was still only 21 when he turned pro with Bev Walker, father Eric continuing to train him, although one win in his first four bouts signalled an underwhelming start to his paid career. But twice in eight days Don picked up retirement victories over Brummie Ian Murray and Sunderland's Alan Storey – although top referee Harry Gibbs caused him a moment's panic on the second occasion. A clash of heads in the seventh left the Welshman bleeding from the scalp and, at the end of the session, Gibbs walked to his corner and announced that he was going to have to stop the fight. Only then did he break into a smile and reveal that Storey had pulled out with a damaged hand!

Don George with Welsh belt

Three points wins followed, including a clear-cut triumph over Newport's future British featherweight king, Steve Sims, who had made a similarly mixed start to life in the paid ranks. Then came the call from West Africa.

Azumah Nelson was not world-famous when George faced him in Accra's Kaneshie Sports Stadium, but the hardcore knew of his talent. A gold medallist at the 1978 Commonwealth Games, he had won all seven as a pro, already acquiring national and African titles. Yet the Swansea man was not fazed.

Accepting that Nelson, who was also four pounds heavier, was the big puncher in the ring, Don focussed on defence, using his jab to keep him at bay and also picking up sufficient points to give him three of the opening four rounds. But the fifth found him on the ropes as Azumah stormed in. Momentarily, George dropped his right arm; it was enough, the local favourite whipping over a left hook that felled Don. He was out for a while after referee Roy Ankrah, a former Commonwealth champion, had completed the count.

He can still see the funny side, though. "When I came round, I was seeing stars," he recalls. "Then I remembered we'd been fighting outdoors!"

On the face of it, George's next foe was rather less formidable. But Ian McLeod had been a useful amateur and had yet to lose a round in his four pro outings; Don managed to win one session when they collided in Glasgow, but was still widely outpointed.

It was time to go home. In what was to be the only time he performed before a Welsh crowd, Don met his third unbeaten opponent on the spin, Cardiffian Mervyn Bennett, at Ebbw Vale Leisure Centre on November 19, 1981. The vacant Welsh feather title was at stake – and Mervyn had already beaten him in a Welsh

Don George has Bennett seeking shelter

ABA final. On a bill which saw kid brother Dave clinch a British flyweight shot, Don completed a family double by edging out the fancied Bennett by half a point on Jim Brimmell's card. George's left landed the cleanest blows on view in a contest that never really caught fire, with the third man frequently forced to separate the combatants. But nobody in the Swansea contingent worried too much when their man's arm was raised at the end.

Don was never to defend. He had broken his right hand so badly that surgeons had to graft bone from his hip to repair it. It was more than 17 months before he returned against Sussex boy Mark West – and the hand went again in the third. The pain forced him to switch to southpaw, which he did well enough to earn the nod. But the Welshman fought just once more.

He travelled to Belgium to face local hero Jean-Marc Renard, whose only defeats had come against Barry McGuigan and, controversially, in Newport, with George victim Sims scraping a disputed decision. There was no argument in Izegem; Renard, to become European champion five months later, knocked George out in four rounds.

With the mitt still a problem, George announced his retirement. After their father fell ill, Don trained brothers David and Eric, but when they packed it in, so did he.

NEIL HADDOCK
(1964–   )

British Super-Featherweight Champion 1992–94

European Super-Featherweight Challenger 1994

Welsh Super-Featherweight Champion 1992

Commonwealth Games Silver Medallist 1986

There's nothing sportswriters like better than a jinx. And when it came to the British super-featherweight championship, they had a belter. Since the adoption of the 9st 4lb division in 1986, 13 people had worn the Lonsdale Belt. Every one of them had lost the title in his first defence. Llanelli southpaw Neil Haddock was 14th in line.

It had been a long road to get that far. He joined Trostre ABC as an enthusiastic 12-year-old and his talent soon earned him a Welsh youth vest. During a four-year stint as an Army driver, he captured national senior honours and matched them in the Combined Services tournament. But the highlight of his amateur career arrived in the Commonwealth Games in 1986.

The field at the Edinburgh event had been decimated by a boycott in protest at the refusal of Prime Minister Margaret Thatcher to support economic sanctions against apartheid-era South Africa. Boxing was particularly hard hit.

There were byes a-plenty and Haddock received one into the semi-final, guaranteeing him a medal before he had even laced on his gloves; the authorities later changed the rules to demand at least one victory. One of the few African nations still competing was Malawi, whose lightweight representative, Byton Mphande, proved no match for Neil, but Asif Dar, a Pakistan-born Canadian, uncorked a left hook in the final and Haddock hit

Neil Haddock

49

the canvas, never likely to beat the count. He still had a silver medal to bring home.

Now back in civvy street, Neil linked up with local manager Glynne Davies, but was soon disabused of any idea that amateur success would guarantee similar joy in the paid ranks. There were more losses than wins in Haddock's first two years and even victory brought its problems: in stopping Kent's Lee Amass, he damaged his left hand so badly that he was out of the ring for 18 months. When he returned, he was pulled out by his corner after South African Paul Ditau Molefyane caught him after the bell. But next time out he floored British ABA champion Mark Ramsey four times en route to a fifth-round triumph.

It earned Neil a shot at Welsh super-feather king Andrew de Abreu, but the Cardiffian was ruled out after the weigh-in, when officials realised that his mandatory suspension following a cut-eye loss did not expire until midnight. Instead, Steve Robinson stepped up as a late, late substitute for what was billed as a final eliminator and won a thriller when Haddock was halted in the ninth with a gash over the right eye which required nine stitches.

The ongoing hand problem sidelined him for several months and, when he did see action, fellow-townsman Barrie Kelley decked him before Neil took the decision, lining up a re-run of that postponed Welsh title tilt at de Abreu. But Andrew came in overweight, was stripped of the crown and Haddock's cuts stoppage win meant nothing.

It was not until May 11, 1992, at Llanelli's Indoor Bowls Centre, that the local favourite tackled former conqueror Robinson for the vacant throne. Steve, by now Welsh champion at nine stone, would have had to decide which belt to keep if he won; Neil saved him the dilemma, but needed a last-round rally to clinch referee Ivor Bassett's verdict. It came just in time. From the early rounds Haddock had been hampered by

Young Neil with a super-cool Colin Jones

facial damage and within seconds of the final bell a grotesque swelling clamped his right eye tight shut.

Dame Fortune seemed to have switched sides. Swansea man Floyd Havard, due to challenge British super-feather boss Michael Armstrong in Bury on October 13, 1992, broke a hand in training and Haddock was called up to replace him at Lancashire town's leisure centre. He was a clear underdog – but he had that jinx in his favour.

No mysterious powers were needed. The Llanelli man's left hooks soon began to trouble the Manchester-based champion, and as early as the second a double left to the jaw left Armstrong draped on the ropes, staring vacantly into the crowd. Somehow the champion survived the session, but the pace was beginning to tell and Michael was a shell by the sixth. Trying to cling on after another knockdown, he seemed to crumple to the canvas. Referee Larry O'Connell at first gestured for him to rise, but then realised the exhausted fighter could no longer do so. Yet again, the super-feather crown had changed hands at the first time of asking.

It was Neil's turn to confront the hoodoo at Oldham Leisure Centre on July 25, 1993, against Mancunian Steve Walker, and the Sunday afternoon crowd witnessed a bit of history. They may have hoped that Walker would become an incredible fifth British ruler for promoter Phil Martin's famous Champs' Camp, but instead had to settle for being on hand as the jinx was finally laid to rest.

Although cut early on, Haddock dropped Walker with a left counter in the sixth and floored him once more in the next. Somehow Steve pulled himself upright, but on shaky legs, and the referee – again Mr O'Connell – had seen enough. For the first time after a British super-feather title fight, the MC was able to announce, "The winner – and STILL champion..."

Haddock had already been named as official challenger to European king Jacobin Yoma, but manager Davies opted for an all-Welsh defence against the patiently waiting Havard. They came face to face at Cardiff's STAR Centre on March 23, 1994. Floyd, little more than eight

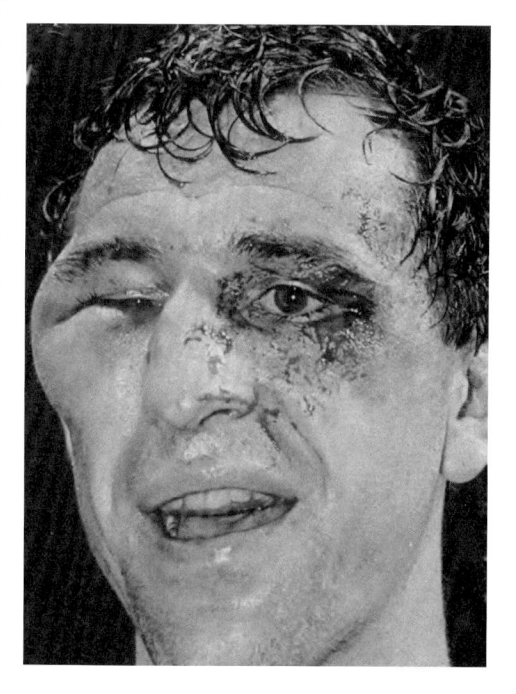

Neil after the second Steve Robinson fight – and he won!

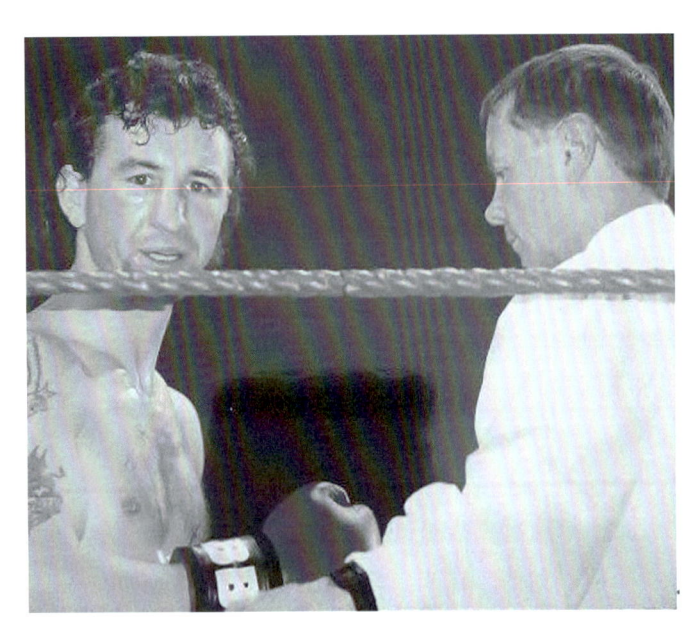

Neil with manager Glynne Davies

weeks after his mauling by world champion 'John-John' Molina, outboxed his fellow-southpaw, his speed and fluency making Haddock seem pedestrian by contrast. Neil tried to force the issue, but even his renowned body blows had little impact on a confident, relaxed challenger.

By the second half of the bout it was largely one-way traffic and referee Roy Francis intervened in the 10th, when a cut above the right eye, damaged in the first, began to bleed more severely.

Despite the loss, Haddock headed for French Guiana to tackle Yoma on May 14, 1993. The concept of a European title fight in South America was somewhat bizarre, but Jacobin had acquired the belt on home turf in Cayenne and was defending it there for the third time. His success was never in doubt. Within a round he had broken Neil's nose and constant pressure convinced the Welshman it would be sensible to stay in his corner after the sixth round. The decision marked not merely his retirement from the contest, but from the ring.

NIGEL HADDOCK
(1966–)

Welsh Featherweight Challenger 1994

Some people are condemned to spend their lives wondering what might have been. Wrong decisions in their teenage years can lead to missed opportunities and squandered talent, particularly among athletes, who, when realisation finally dawns, are generally too old to make up the wasted time.

When you consider how much of Nigel Haddock's young life was effectively lost in a haze of drink and drugs, it is incredible that he achieved so much. If he had shown the discipline and dedication of older brother Neil, he might well have matched him in collecting a Lonsdale Belt.

Nigel was a teenager when he turned pro with Glynne Davies, while Neil was still chasing amateur honours. A debut defeat in Birmingham was followed by an unbeaten streak lasting six fights and culminating in the big right hand which brought a two-round demolition of Cardiffian Tony Rahman on the same day that big brother was clinching a place in the Commonwealth Games final.

Three successive victories, including an injury stoppage of US-based Dubliner Richie Foster – the previous man to halt the Irish boxer was Freddie Roach, now a world-class trainer – and suddenly the Haddock name was being mentioned on the Continent. It was the Italians, particularly, who picked out Nigel as a likely lad to test their stars. Down south in Calabria he was outpointed by locally based Dominican Freddy Cruz, later to challenge Cardiff's Steve Robinson for the WBO feather title. When he returned, it was in the north, where he was forced to retire after three rounds against unbeaten Maurizio Stecca; two months later the Italian was wearing the WBO belt.

Back in Britain, Haddock drew with Kevin Pritchard, who was to become British super-

Nigel Haddock

Eyes closed, Nigel awaits a right from Harris

feather boss before the year was out, but then found South African champion Paul Ditau Molefyane too tall, too heavy and far too talented as he went down to a wide 10-round reverse; Molefyane flew to Britain soon afterwards and completed the double by halting brother Neil.

The younger Haddock's relationship with mentor Davies had been an on-off affair, Glynne frequently turfing him out as repeated drug use brought regular encounters with the law. At the start of 1990, former world title contender Colin Jones attempted to stem the tide, but to no avail and the Board of Control pulled Nigel's licence. It was nearly three years before he boxed again.

Inspired by Neil's accession to the British super-feather throne, Nigel resolved to get his act together. Davies agreed to take him back and when he passed a drugs test set up by the Board, he was given the green light to resume his career. He certainly made an impressive entrance, climbing through the ropes at the Welsh Institute of Sport wearing a white sunhat, which he removed to reveal a Mohican haircut before battering North Walian Eddie Lloyd into retirement after four rounds, his left eye swollen and bleeding.

A year later, the resurrected Llanelli man was matched with Swansea redhead Peter Harris for the vacant Welsh feather title, topping a dinner show on May 20, 1994, at the Glyn Clydach Hotel on the outskirts of Neath. It was one of those fights which occasionally underline how deceptive appearances can be. Anyone arriving late and seeing Harris in the ring, blood pouring down each side of his face, with a further gash on the bridge of his nose, would be forgiven for assuming they were looking at the loser. Then they would have noticed that he was smiling – and parading the belt.

Peter, six years after ruling Britain's nine-stone men for 84 days, split his right eyebrow in a second-round head clash and twice referee Ivor Bassett took him to the corner before allowing him to continue; fearing that the next inspection might prove the last, he began to look for a knockout. But Haddock was durable, while Harris lacked power and his all-out attacks took more out of him than his opponent. Nigel began to claw back the early deficit, but the ringwise Harris began to skip around the ring, occasionally showboating, in a bid to convince the Llanelli man that he had plenty in the tank.

As the fight moved into the closing rounds, Peter, realising it would be allowed to run its course, went back to his jab and even a new wound over his left eye midway through the last came too late to rob him of victory. But Nigel had played his part in an enthralling tussle which kept the sell-out crowd on edge throughout.

There was little left for Haddock. Unbeaten Seoul Olympian Dave Anderson floored and outpointed him – that was perhaps to be expected – but when he was cut and clearly outscored in front of his hometown crowd by Pembroke journeyman Steve Burton it was a shock. Nigel got the message and called it a day.

There were sporadic struggles with his old demons, but determination – and a new religious belief – helped him get back on the right path. These days he uses his experiences as a volunteer at a centre for the homeless.

CERI HALL
(1980–)

- **Celtic Light-Welterweight Champion 2007**
- **EU Light-Welterweight Challenger 2006**

Every son wants to do better than his father. Keith Hall had reached the Welsh ABA bantamweight final in 1974, only to go down on points to Tre-Ivor's Pat Mullins. Son Ceri, having followed Dad to Penyrheol ABC, boxed his way to four finals – and won the lot.

The Loughor bricklayer represented Wales at the 1998 Commonwealth Games, losing a decision to the Pakistani who went on to claim silver, but when personal problems forced him to withdraw from the Four Nations squad four years later, the authorities left him out of that summer's Manchester event. Hall, who had felt he was in with a good chance of a medal, promptly turned pro with Paul Boyce.

His new life began spectacularly when he despatched fellow-debutant Martin Turner in just 67 seconds at Swansea Leisure Centre – he floored him with his first punch as a paid fighter – but Hall was soon introduced to one of the fight game's traditional hazards, the difficulty of persuading local referees that you have beaten the hometown hero in a close contest. Back in Wales, Ceri was the man having his arm raised, but travel was unavoidable when he was given an unexpected title shot. When a proposed scrap fell through, manager Boyce put out feelers for an alternative payday and came up with a date in Italy involving the vacant EU light-welter belt.

Ceri Hall

The other corner in the Eternal City on March 25, 2006 – Hall's 26th birthday – held Giorgio Marinelli, a Roman whose 13 straight successes had already brought him a couple of minor IBF honours. By now Colin Jones had taken over Hall's training, although the fighter's father was still involved, but even the presence of a three-time world title challenger in the corner made no difference.

"I reckon I won the first," recalls Ceri, "but, to be honest, I don't think I won any after that!"

'The Shark of Torre Angelo' had still lost only once when his career was ended by a road accident in 2008; by then, Hall, too, had retired. But not before claiming a title of his own.

Not that he was in the best of form when opportunity knocked. Ceri was outsmarted by former England amateur Michael Grant, raising eyebrows when he was booked to face Scot Stuart Green for the vacant Celtic light-welter crown on the Gammer-Williams undercard at Neath Leisure Centre on March 2, 2007. But Hall finally showed what was capable of.

Job done – Hall turns away from a beaten Green

An early right from Green had him flexing his jaw as if to check it was in one piece, but the Loughor man soon assumed control of the centre of the ring and his jab brought blood from Stuart's nose. The Scot was soon marked beneath the left eye as Ceri kept busy, responding to an isolated uppercut with a series of his own. Hall took a little time off in the middle rounds, allowing Green to narrow the deficit, but the tiring Fifer was docked a point by referee Richie Davies for a rabbit punch in the eighth. The sudden ending was, nevertheless, unexpected.

Ceri opened the ninth with a heavy left and, as Stuart tottered, threw a perfectly timed right through the middle. Down went Green and, although he regained the vertical, his unsteady legs prompted the third man to wave it off. Manager Boyce, whose brainwave led to the introduction of the Celtic belts, could celebrate his first champion.

Three months later Hall was back at the same venue to defend against Port Talbot steelworker Stuart Phillips. It was a memorable encounter, with the holder boxing as well as he had ever done in the early stages. Phillips was soon marked up on both cheeks, while a nick over Ceri's left eye, caused by a head clash, never posed a problem. A cracking right hand jolted Stuart at the start of the sixth and the title seemed likely to stay put.

But everything changed in the eighth. Hall's dominance continued for the first two minutes, but then Phillips whipped home a sharp right to the head and Ceri found himself looking up as referee Roddy Evans counted. He made it to his feet, but walked into a whirlwind, a vicious left to the body sending him over again. Somehow he arose and the bell came to his rescue. The ninth saw toe-to-toe exchanges as Stuart strove to repeat his success, but by the last he had run out of steam and Ceri, with a left beneath the ribs, had him in difficulty.

This time it was Stuart glad to hear the gong, especially as he was rewarded with the decision by a single point. As both recovered in their respective dressing rooms – the exhausted new champion needing some precautionary oxygen – each praised the other as the hardest man he had ever faced.

It was a pretty good way to leave the scene. Ceri hung up his gloves and later joined mentor Jones as a coach at Penyrheol, stepping up as the main man when Colin took over the national squad.

MICHAEL HARRIS
(1964–   )

- **Commonwealth Light-Middleweight Challenger 1989**
- **British Light-Welterweight Challenger 1986**
- **British Light-Middleweight Challenger 1988**
- **Welsh Light-Welterweight Champion 1984–87**
- **Welsh Light-Middleweight Champion 1989–91**

They often warn about fighting away from home against the promoter's prospect, suggesting the visitor will receive few favours. When Michael Harris signed up for a shot at the vacant Welsh light-middleweight championship, at the STAR Centre in Cardiff on St David's Day 1989, he went one step further: he was booked to swap punches with the promoter himself.

Kevin Hayde had sorted himself a title shot on his first show, but while the business side was satisfactory, he found the fight less so. Faulty scales had left Harris with a stone to shed in the last week and he needed two attempts before making the 11st limit. But Michael, who had stopped the Cardiffian as an amateur, settled quickly behind his left jab, establishing a points advantage. Staggered in the sixth, Harris was never seriously troubled thereafter, although the effort of weight-making had him blowing hard. Referee Roddy Evans rewarded him by a single-round margin.

It made Portmead boy Harris a two-weight champion. Trained by father Gordon, Michael was a decent amateur who turned pro at 18 after failing to make the 1982 Commonwealth Games

Michael Harris

squad. He won 13 of his first 14 contests, but was still only 19 when he ascended the vacant light-welter throne with a points decision over former holder Ray Price at the Afan Lido on June 13, 1984. It was a disappointing contest: only when the younger man relaxed in the later stages did he begin to score consistently, but it was enough for referee Ivor Bassett, who gave him the nod by half a point.

Harris kept on winning, although he had a problem with Scots called Dave – his first three defeats came at the hands of Messrs Savage, McCabe and Douglas, all Caledonians named after Wales's patron saint. There was also a points loss in Copenhagen to locally based Ugandan Mohammed Kawoya.

But the Board of Control matched the Welshman with Midlander Tony McKenzie, a man he had already beaten, in an eliminator for the British light-welter crown. After 10 close rounds on a dinner show in Solihull, opinion was divided as to the winner. Nobody expected referee Larry O'Connell to have given Michael just one round.

The victor went on to knock out namesake Clinton McKenzie for the vacant title and, just five weeks later, put it on the line against Harris at Stevenage on October 25, 1986. Michael came in a pound and a half heavy at the first attempt, and it took its toll on his stamina.

Even though the challenger's defensive ability kept McKenzie at bay early on – apart from a tough second session – he began to ship body shots as the contest moved past halfway. Harris had to cling on to survive the ninth and the next brought the end. Two left hooks sent the Welshman flying, his head striking the bottom rope; by the time he regained his feet the count had been completed.

The Swansea man was almost a stone heavier when he reappeared seven months later to spoil the comeback of former British welter king Kostas Petrou, while a trip to Madrid brought a "draw" against recently dethroned European champion Alfonso Redondo before Michael, now definitively a light-middle, was given another shot at a Lonsdale Belt.

He was called in to face Southern Area ruler Gary Cooper for the vacant title at Wembley Grand Hall on February 3, 1988. For a brief moment in the fifth, it looked as though Michael might upset the odds, a solid left hook depositing the Hampshire veteran on his backside, but he was shaken rather than stunned and clambered up at two. Cooper's left jab had generally kept the shorter man at bay and, although Harris controlled the middle sessions, Gary restored the earlier pattern and Mickey Vann favoured him by a somewhat generous four-round margin.

It was to be Michael's last outing in England. He fished out his passport to visit South Africa, Spain and France, losing all three bouts on points, though the Madrid crowd booed the verdict in favour of old foe Redondo and French gipsy Pierre-Frank Winterstein scraped through via majority decision.

Manager Colin Breen began campaigning for another crack at Cooper, but Harris had to settle for the Welsh title victory over Hayde before being offered a last chance at international glory. It required a long journey to Ettalong, a resort on the New South Wales coast, where Michael challenged Commonwealth light-middle boss Troy Waters on May 26, 1989.

Michael boxes an exhibition with the legendary Roberto Duran

Arriving a couple of weeks before the fight, he found no training facilities had been provided and no sparring partners. But he still began confidently against the tall Sydneysider and seemed to be ahead when disaster struck in the eighth.

Waters finally landed a solid shot, but became wild in his attempts to end matters and Harris survived the session – or so he thought. The bell rang, but Waters landed two more punches as Michael lowered his hands. The recipient told referee Trevor Christian that he was OK and went back to his corner. Beer cans were hurled into the ring and it became clear that the fight was over.

Referee Christian insisted he had not heard the gong. When Harris raised his arm and turned away, he had taken it as a gesture of retirement. As the Aussie fans celebrated, there was no way the decision could be changed. For Michael, increasingly disillusioned with the way the sport was run, it was the final straw. While Waters went on to three world title bids – all unsuccessful – the Swansea man helped out for a while in the Breen gym, training former victim Price and Commonwealth Games rep Mark Flynn among others, before drifting away from the game for good.

PETER HARRIS
(1962–   )

- **British Featherweight Champion 1988**
- **Welsh Featherweight Champion 1986–91, 1994–96**

Boxers are famously alone once the bell rings. But victory is still not entirely down to them. Peter Harris became British champion thanks to a man sitting at the back of the hall. Ernie Fossey, a useful lightweight in his day, had become one of the game's top matchmakers, but he had another specialized talent: he could repair cuts.

Harris had been due to challenge former stablemate Robert Dickie for the British featherweight crown, but the holder pulled out and was stripped, the Board calling up Lancastrian southpaw Kevin Taylor to face Peter for the vacant title. They met at the Afan Lido on February 24, 1988.

It was so nearly over in the first round. Harris stormed out, catching Kevin cold and sending him reeling around the ring, desperately trying to fend off the red-haired hurricane. But before the session had ended, a clash of heads left Peter with blood streaming from his left eyebrow. Trainer Colin Jones had plenty of experience of such injuries, but as victim rather than physician, and struggled to stem the flow before round two.

But help was at hand. The off-duty Fossey, having settled back to relax and enjoy the action, saw the situation, raced to the dressing-room for his kit and was able to take over in the next interval. He had some extra work when Taylor's head-down approach caused another injury above Harris's right ear, but, thanks to Ernie's skill, neither wound distracted Peter from the job in hand.

Peter Harris

The sharper puncher, he built a substantial lead over the Rochdale southpaw, although Kevin's two coachloads of fans had something to cheer as he battled back in the sixth and seventh, landing roundhouse punches on the suddenly wary Welshman. By the ninth, however, Peter was back in charge; Taylor, a large swelling enveloping his right cheek, was starting to fade. When Harris responded to another billy-goat onslaught with a deliberate butt of his own, referee Adrian Morgan lectured both men. But, despite a desperate last-ditch effort from Taylor, Peter was four rounds clear at the final bell and the Lonsdale Belt was staying in Wales.

It was the culmination of a career which began at eight, when father Gordon took the Portmead youngster to the gym, hoping the exercise would help clear up a chest complaint. It worked – and in due course it became clear that he had a natural talent which took him to a Welsh schools title and a runner-up spot in the senior championships. Kid brother Michael turned pro first, but it was the obvious course for Peter, too, and he joined the expanding Colin Breen camp.

He lost his first bout – just as he had as an amateur – but was unbeaten in his next seven, culminating in the triumph that first brought him to the notice of the world beyond Wales. Harris faced fast-rising Keith Wallace, already Commonwealth champion, at the Afan Lido, capitalising on the Scouser's sluggish start to take a disputed decision from referee Adrian Morgan. When Peter's arm was raised, his brother, who won a Welsh title an hour later, ran to ringside to congratulate him – in his underpants!

Suddenly, Harris was a wanted man. And he cashed in, at the expense of his record. There was a trip to the Bahamas to face local hero Ray Minus, Jr, followed by dates with Central Area champion John Farrell, British bantam boss John Feeney and, in Grenoble, with European fly king Antoine Montero. All ended in points defeats, though he floored Minus, went down by half-point margins against the two Englishmen and persuaded one French judge that he had done enough to beat Montero.

Peter's bantamweight dreams died when he was two pounds overweight for a British title final eliminator against Ulsterman Roy Webb, rendering pointless his stoppage victory. Faced with a move to feather, Peter left Breen, whose focus at nine stone was mainly on Dickie, linking up with Alan Davies and a new trainer in Nigel Page. His was immediately named to contest the vacant Welsh throne against someone making a bigger leap in weight, Kelvin Smart, a former British champion down at flyweight. When they met at the Patti Pavilion on November 18, 1986, Peter took nine rounds and shared the other, his body punching – not all legal, although Smart never complained – making the difference.

The Board nominated Peter for another final eliminator at his new weight and he travelled to Solihull to face former foe Farrell. Now with local superstar Jones in the corner, his greater workrate was rewarded by London referee Larry O'Connell after a contest that never caught fire.

Peter's triumph against Taylor made him the sixth Welshman to wear the feather crown, but his reign was to be the shortest – less than three months. Lying in wait was an unbeaten Liverpool lad called Paul Hodkinson. Yet it was Harris who made the early impact at a packed Afan Lido on May 18, 1988. 'Hoko' was constantly out of range, his strange habit of tugging at his shorts hardly helping him find any fluency. By the fifth, however, the Scouser began to turn the tide, a left hook staggering the champion. As the bout moved into its second half, Peter was beginning to blow, while a cut near his right eyebrow proved a distraction.

It was one-way traffic by the eighth. Harris was forced to retreat, needing the bell to rescue him after being dropped by a left hook in the 10th. Exhaustion, as much as power, sent Peter back to the canvas early in the 12th and, although he rose gamely, referee O'Connell stepped in.

'Hoko' added the European belt before returning to the Lido on September 6, 1989, to give Peter another shot. The Swansea man had not thrown a punch since their first meeting 16 months earlier. He had, however, spent a month in camp on Gower and started well, holding his own for the first five rounds and finding Hodkinson surprisingly easy to hit. As in their previous encounter, Paul came on strong after halfway and Harris found himself defending desperately. At the end of the seventh, he shook his head as he returned to the corner. The writing was on the wall.

When the Welshman emerged from a close-quarter exchange with blood pouring from his right eyebrow, referee John Coyle had seen enough and waved the fight off. Hodkinson went on to wear the WBC crown, while Peter took a long break before returning in 1991 with Mike Copp looking after training.

He lost his Welsh feather title to Cardiffian Steve Robinson – a verdict he still protests – and crossed gloves with some of the best men around: future European champion Stéphane Haccoun,

Peter unloads on Paul Hodkinson

former Commonwealth king Paul Harvey and two-time British titleholder Jon Jo Irwin all beat him on points.

There was a bright spot when Harris regained the Welsh nine-stone honour with a clear decision over Llanelli's Nigel Haddock at the Glyn Clydach Hotel above Neath on May 20, 1994, a bout which ended with the winner's face a mask of blood.

In a challenge for the WBO Penta-Continental strap in Cardiff, all three judges gave the nod to holder Wilson Docherty – "You must get points for hitting the air these days," said a baffled Breen, back in the Harris corner – but Peter went to Glasgow and gained revenge in a final eliminator for his old British title, referee John Coyle favouring him by half a point.

He never had another chance at the Lonsdale Belt. With the title clash already booked, he travelled to South Africa and was stopped by former IBF super-bantam boss Welcome Ncita; when he arrived home he found the Board were insisting on him "proving himself" before facing new ruler Irwin. Disgusted, Peter chased the cheques, fighting another ex-world champion, Jimmi Bredahl, in Denmark and, finally, future

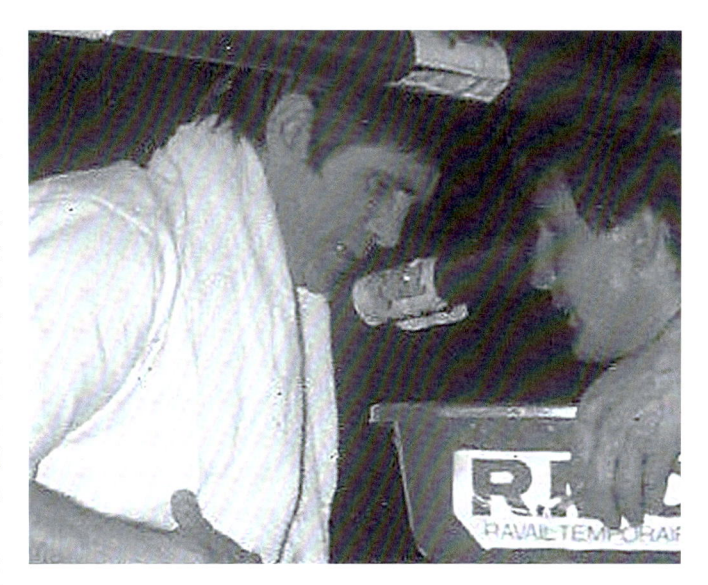

Jim Bromfield imparts his wisdom to Peter ...

... and Peter Harris passes it on to son Jay

IBF champion Cassius Baloyi in Manchester. Both defeats, but financially beneficial.

It was enough. At 34, it was time to pack it in. But when son Jay showed an interest, Dad began to train him and has seen the chip off the old block turn into a useful prospect in the pro ranks.

FLOYD HAVARD
(1965–)

- British Super-Featherweight Champion 1988–89, 1994–95
- IBF Super-Featherweight Challenger 1994

With a name like Floyd, the youngster from the Swansea Valley pit village of Craigcefnparc was always destined for the ring. His father, Howard, was a big fan of former world heavyweight champion Patterson and endowed his son – born a few weeks before the New Yorker's unsuccessful challenge to Muhammad Ali – with his idol's forename.

But true inspiration came from someone closer to home: Colin Jones, then still an amateur. The 10-year-old Havard joined his hero's Penyrheol ABC and trainer Gareth Bevan, collecting a cupboardful of junior trophies and a British ABA title, while experiencing a taste of the big time when he flew to Las Vegas to watch his former clubmate in his second showdown with Milton McCrory.

There was no such glamour in Floyd's first years as a pro under rising young manager Frank Warren. The young southpaw had to serve his apprenticeship in the small halls and leisure centres of Britain. But 18 straight wins – the last four over American imports – earned him a crack at the British super-feather crown worn by Midlander Pat Cowdell, twice a world title challenger.

Warren staged the clash at the Afan Lido on May 18, 1988, with the holder, nearing 35, on the brink of history: victory would make him the first man to win a Lonsdale Belt outright at two different weights. Havard, a dozen years younger, had never met anyone in this class. It showed in the early exchanges, with Floyd seemingly at a loss how

Floyd Havard with trainer Gareth Bevan

Floyd lands a right on the incoming Cowdell

to deal with the combinations coming his way from a man who had won an Olympic bronze when Floyd was still in short pants.

But time catches up with the best. By the midway point, Pat, despite a handy lead, was beginning to flag, a body shot leaving its mark as the Warley fighter's grip on the title began to slip. The effort needed to earn a share of the seventh left him struggling at the start of the eighth, with Havard, still comparatively fresh, determined to seize the chance.

The Welshman stormed in, placing no fewer than 16 precise punches to the head before the veteran dropped to his haunches. He dragged himself up at seven, but referee Larry O'Connell saw there was nothing left and called a halt, Pat's nod acknowledging the correctness of his decision. Cowdell took the ring microphone to wish his conqueror well, while announcing his own retirement.

It should have meant lift-off for the new ruler, but the boxing fates had different plans. Another two Americans were beaten, but on both occasions at the expense of knuckle damage to his right hand. It was still a problem when Havard made his first defence against fading former champion John Doherty in the same hall on September 6, 1989.

Floyd built an early lead, but his troublesome right let him down again in the fourth. Perhaps a switch to orthodox might have helped, but his Yorkshire rival was constantly harrying him and the contest began to turn. Havard was under non-stop pressure, but it was still something of a surprise when, less than a minute into the 11th, he turned away, shaking his hand and informing referee John Coyle that he could not continue.

A surgeon at Morriston Hospital grafted bone from his hip on to the fragile knuckles, but it was 18 months before Floyd returned to the ring.

Floyd batters two-time Commonwealth champion Thunder Ayeh

Floored by Tony Foster in the first of his comeback fight and also down against Harry Escott, he recovered to win both in a run of five victories which prompted his new promoter, Frank Maloney, to bring Puerto Rican IBF champion 'John-John' Molina to Cardiff on January 22, 1994. It proved a bridge too far.

After one exploratory round, Molina stepped up a gear and the gulf in class became obvious. Havard took a knee in the third and the end looked imminent, but craggy trainer Lou Duva was cautioning the champion to take his time and allow the Welshman to put on a show for the crowd at the Institute of Sport. At the end of the fifth, he gave 'John-John' the green light; Floyd, his nose broken, was floored again and retired in the corner after six chastening sessions.

Pundits and punters were writing him off, but Havard bounced back just two months later to regain his British title. Llanelli's stylish Neil Haddock had made the first successful defence in the hoodoo-blighted 9st 4lb division, but a second was beyond his reach. The battle of southpaws at Cardiff's STAR Centre was unexpectedly one-sided, Floyd dominating throughout, and when a cut above Haddock's right eye became increasingly problematic in the 10th, referee Roy Francis called it off.

Late stoppages of Scot Dave McHale and former holder Michael Armstrong earned Havard a Lonsdale Belt to keep, at which point he vacated the position. There followed three more victories before a recurring ankle injury sidelined him, costing a shot at Colombian Wilson Palacio for the vacant WBO throne. Cardiffian Barry Jones replaced his fellow-countryman and defeated Palacio; Floyd never boxed again.

There were comeback attempts, real and rumoured, one taking him as far as ringside at a Leicester Square nightclub only for a wide discrepancy in the weights to scupper the bout. He eventually reappeared on the unlicensed circuit, winning an alleged British title at the age of 44, while a variety of day jobs included a spell as a trainer and agent in Ukraine. Nowadays Floyd travels the world as a maintenance man on cruise liners.

World traveller Floyd visits Canada

GARETH HOWELLS
(1948–1991)

🥊 Welsh Bantamweight Challenger 1970, 1971

When Gareth James Howells turned up at Llangennech ABC to learn the Noble Art, he had no difficulty remembering the name of his coach: he was also called Gareth James Howells!

Luckily, the boxer was more generally known as 'Guzz', so that problem was solved. And he also showed enough talent to keep his namesake happy, wearing a Welsh vest (as did brother Vince) and reaching a Welsh ABA final, where he lost on points to Les Pickett. The watching Eddie Thomas was sufficiently impressed to offer him a contract.

Howells, trained by his father, Ivor, at the White Hart gym in Llanelli, launched his pro career with an explosive one-round demolition job on Manchester's Tommy Moore at London's National Sporting Club, prompting *Boxing News* to comment that "Thomas looks to have found another lively one". But they pronounced him "less impressive" when he returned to the elegant Café Royal a fortnight later, even though he outpointed fellow-Welshman Tony Williams.

The Pontlottyn man was to gain his revenge the following month on the Howard Winstone-José Legrá undercard at Porthcawl, but it was down to a cut eye, as was Gareth's second loss, but whenever he avoided injury

Gareth Howells (right) challenges Colin Miles

Gareth enjoyed the spoils of his excellent technical skills, with four successive decisions going his way, including the conquest of future Commonwealth title challenger John Kellie.

As a reward for his winning run, Howells found himself facing Rhondda fighter Colin Miles for the vacant Welsh bantam crown, before a packed house at Swansea's Top Rank Suite on June 22, 1970.

It took Miles a few sessions to come to terms with his foe's southpaw stance, but as he settled, the Tonyrefail man began to land his own leads, with a right cross to the head providing back-up. Gareth was nicked over the right eye in the third, but it never became a factor. He kept marching forward, firing rights to head and body, yet by the sixth was beginning to display the evidence of Miles's attentions.

Midway through the seventh Howells was under fire sufficiently to take a count of eight and he was on the receiving end for the rest of the session. With an injured left hand reducing his ability to keep Colin at bay, Gareth was pulled out in the interval.

Despite a points loss in a rematch with Kellie, by now Scottish champion, Howells was given a second crack at Miles on February 22, 1971, at the Afan Lido. 'Guzz' was in top shape and displayed plenty of skill, but found it hard to hold off the non-stop aggression of the Rhondda fighter. Early on, Howells often beat Colin to the punch and used his fast footwork to escape retribution, but by halfway he was feeling the pace. Ace cutman Thomas dealt with a nick over Gareth's left eye, but could do nothing about his pupil's waning energy. The challenger found sufficient vim to stand toe-to-toe in the last round, but referee Jim Brimmell had Miles three rounds clear at the end.

A third meeting was scheduled for October 1971, although the title was not to be at stake, but Colin had to pull out after breaking a finger in drawing with Ulsterman Paddy Graham a few weeks earlier. Ironically, Graham was the man in the corner opposite Howells a month later, dropping and outscoring the Llanelli man at the Midland Sporting Club in Solihull – and that was to be the last action of Gareth's career. At just 23, disillusioned by a combination of injuries and short-notice fights, he called it a day.

He had a variety of jobs before turning his hand to pulling pints at the Brecon Arms in his home town, later becoming landlord at the Bell in Bynea. But while he was working on the demolition of an oil tank at a Milford Haven refinery the structure collapsed, killing him instantly.

CHRIS JACOBS
(1961–   )

Welsh Heavyweight Champion 1985–91

Not many former prop forwards can say they spent a month in Canada sparring with Lennox Lewis. But the Llanelli cabbie's claims to fistic fame are based on more than mere reflected glory.

After all, in theory he is still the national heavyweight champion, in that nobody has contested the belt for a quarter of a century.

Chris Jacobs learned the basics with Gareth Howells at Trostre ABC, claiming a Welsh ABA super-heavyweight title in 1983, going down to Londoner Keith Ferdinand in the British semi-finals. A year later he had turned pro with the Colin Breen stable. Within four fights he was the top man in Wales.

After two wins, followed by a draw with the ordinary Gipsy Carman, Jacobs was matched with Risca's Andrew Gerrard for the vacant Welsh crown. They met at the Newport Centre on September 25, 1985, one of two title fights on a card promoted by Gerrard's manager, Billy May.

The local man was vastly more experienced, with an itinerary that had taken him to Germany, Italy, France and the Ivory Coast. It was no surprise that Andrew was a clear favourite.

But Jacobs, having shed more than a stone since the Carman fight, was unexpectedly six pounds lighter than his foe, and his greater mobility – coupled with his southpaw stance – proved the decisive factor. One round was much like the next, Chris repeating the same, simple combination of a southpaw lead, followed by a left to the face. Despite its predictability, the ponderous Gerrard was unable to deal with it other than by holding.

Only when Jacobs began to tire in the closing sessions did Andrew initiate anything much in the way of attacks and by then it was too late. Rhondda referee Ivor Bassett had the West Walian four rounds in front.

Chris Jacobs

Instead of moving towards a possible British title shot, Chris began to seek more lucrative paydays on the Continent. His Grand Tour began well, with a cuts win in Italy over Argentinian champion Daniel Falconi, who had lost only once in 19 contests, but then reality took over.

Former Olympian and future world cruiser king Anaclet Wamba took a points verdict, as did another Europe-based African, unbeaten Zambian Michael Simuwelu, while South African titleholder Pierre Coetzer knocked out Jacobs in Johannesburg. When he stayed at home, Geordie Paul Lister outscored him, while former British champion Trevor Hughroy Currie won in two rounds.

Things improved with a victory in Belgium and then over Londoner Barry Ellis, but there followed three straight points defeats, with the French gipsy, future European ruler Jean-Baptiste Chanet, among his conquerors. But domestically there was only one rival around: that man Gerrard.

They met again to dispute Welsh supremacy on June 8, 1989, at Cardiff's STAR Centre. Since their first encounter Gerrard had also lost more than he had won, while adding Danish and Australian stamps to his passport. But once again many thought he would prevail.

A packed house watched 10 gruelling rounds in which Jacobs, again six pounds lighter, repeated his earlier triumph, this time by two rounds on the card of Pontypool referee Roddy Evans. Despite the raucous encouragement of his legion of fans, Andrew again found Chris's wrong-way-round stance difficult to combat and the Llanelli man's more solid and accurate blows earned the verdict.

Jacobs returned to the STAR to avenge an earlier loss by knocking

Jacobs with trainer Jimmy Bromfield

out future promoter Jess Harding, but that was the last time his arm was raised. He was more or less retired – at least in his mind – by the time former British cruiser boss Tee Jay demolished him in five, while Herbie Hide, later to win the WBO heavyweight belt, did the job inside a round.

There were a few more seasons in the pack for Furnace and the taxi firm gave way in due course to a small garage, while the excitement of the ring was replaced by work as a part-time fireman.

Chris avoids a right from Jess Harding

DOUG JAMES
(1958–   )

🥊 Welsh Middleweight Champion 1983–85

It all began with a knockabout game of rugby, throwing a can about on Swansea Beach. The 18-year-old Doug James and his two mates found they were blowing a bit and decided they needed to work on their fitness. So they headed for the Swansea RAOB gym in Wind Street, where, almost inevitably, they were encouraged to box.

The guiding light there at the time was former champion Jackie Kiley, who inspired the teenage scaffolder from Gendros to take the sport seriously. In due course, young James wore a Welsh international vest and claimed the 1979 Welsh ABA title, flooring Bristolian Nick Wilshire before being halted in the British final. It was time to get paid for his punches.

As a new recruit to the Colin Breen camp, James soon made an impression, the only reverse in his first 10 bouts coming on cuts. But potential opponents began to shy away and Doug was inactive for a full year before a trip up to Scotland brought a narrow defeat to local southpaw Billy Lauder, while Yorkshireman Brian Anderson also prevailed over eight rounds. There were a couple more wins, including revenge over Lauder, before disaster struck.

Mark Kaylor, resplendent in West Ham colours, had won all 16 since turning pro following the Moscow Olympics. In front of his East End disciples at the York Hall, he was always expected to extend that tally and Doug, whose preparations had been less than ideal, never looked likely to spoil the party.

Doug James

He landed a couple of solid rights late in the opener, but a lump was already forming below James's left eye and Kaylor's punches, methodical rather than spectacular, added a split lip in the second. A double left hook, supplemented by a short right, dropped Doug, who rose at one, something he did again when another right returned him to the canvas. A third knockdown, even though the brave Welshman clambered up again, prompted referee Sid Nathan to end matters.

After the Kaylor defeat, James, still only 24, announced his retirement. But as the bruises faded, his enthusiasm returned and his decision to try again was encouraged by the offer of a shot at the vacant Welsh middleweight belt.

He was given home advantage at the Top Rank Suite on January 28, 1983, with journeyman Winston Burnett nominated for the other corner. Burnett was a somewhat surprising choice, having lost 10 in a row, most recently a five-round stoppage at the hands of Midlander Cordwell Hylton two months earlier, when the Cardiff man scaled 12st 8lb.

To nobody's great surprise, Winston found the task of making middleweight impossible and was replaced at a few days' notice by stablemate Horace McKenzie, a former national champion at welterweight. The late change made little difference to James, who was in command throughout. The hometown hero carried by far the harder punch and it was demonstrated as early as the second, when a left stunned Horace. The Cardiffian's efforts to fight back were praiseworthy, but ineffectual, while James's responses were having a visible effect. The Jamaican-born McKenzie was reduced to claiming his tormentor, but still threw enough in return to keep referee Ivor Bassett at bay.

Doug celebrates his Welsh title win with manager Colin Breen (left) and John Parry

But the Rhondda official took a close look at the end of the eighth and when Horace was floored midway through the ninth, he had seen enough. Three months after his painful experience at the hands of the relentless Kaylor, James was a national champion.

Among those at ringside for the McKenzie fight were former world champion Alan Minter and his manager and father-in-law, Doug Bidwell, and, with his contract with Breen at an end, the two Dougs linked up. As a result, James never again boxed in Wales, let alone defended his crown.

His tour of distant parts began well enough, a trip to Aberdeen bringing an eighth-round victory over unbeaten prospect Cameron Lithgow, but the celebratory feeling did not last.

Sheffield's Anderson, a points winner 18 months earlier, came in as a two-day substitute on a London dinner show and dismissed Doug with a single left hook in just 30 seconds. Six weeks later, the highly touted Errol Christie, back from two wins in the US, flattened the Welshman in four on a Saturday afternoon bill in Coventry, live on ITV's *World of Sport*.

James did end the year with a draw against Brentford's T.P. Jenkins, but a rematch ended in the unbeaten Londoner's favour in the seventh. There was brief encouragement for Doug when he climbed off the floor in the first to knock out Leicester's Johnny Elliott in four, but that was his last experience of success.

A points loss in Toulouse to Frenchman Pierre Joly – a future European champion – was followed by another against middle-of-the-road Londoner Conrad Oscar. And when Frenchman Pierre-Frank Winterstein, already a quick winner over old foe McKenzie, repeated the dose against James it signalled the end of the road.

It was not merely his last fight, it was his last involvement with boxing. Beyond the ropes he has worked in various council jobs: there were 20 years dealing with adults with learning difficulties, as well as other areas of social services and even a year as a traffic warden. Now Doug is driving lorries. But not to the gym.

RONNIE JAMES
(1917–1977)

🥊 British Lightweight Champion 1944–1947

As the angelic voice of a boy soprano soared about the chapel, few of the adoring mothers gazing from the pews could have realised that behind that innocent face lay a burning desire to fight. But as young Ronnie James collected a succession of prizes at local eisteddfodau his thoughts were more on emulating his idols: Jim Driscoll, Freddie Welsh and Jimmy Wilde.

It was his shopkeeper father, David, an amateur boxer himself, who sparked this enthusiasm for the ring. Worried that his musical activities might lead to bullying by the more philistine of Ronnie's contemporaries, he decided to check out the lad's ability to look after himself. Having taken him up to the loft above the store, he invited Ronnie to hit him. The force of the blow he duly received convinced James senior of one thing: "You can do all the singing you like," he told his son. "But you're going to be a boxer!"

So, each day, after delivering the groceries, the Bonymaen lad would be despatched to Dai Curvis's gym to learn the rudiments of his new craft. He learned quickly and the wins came thick and fast.

There were lessons outside the ring, too. After he marked his 17th birthday by outpointing Brummie Harry Edwards, his mother rewarded him with a glass of port. Ronnie was so ill he missed the party!

The star of the Curvis stable at the time was Len Beynon, a Welsh champion at bantam and, later, featherweight. James

Ronnie James

was still under 18 when he was deemed ready to tackle Beynon at Swansea's Vetch Field, on a day so wet the referee wore a mac and a bowler hat. At the end the official strode through the rain to lift the youngster's arm. The gym – and Swansea – had a new hero.

A draw with former British bantam champion Dick Corbett underlined James's progress. Soon one of the fight world's great names was to be convinced. In January 1936, boxing historian Nat Fleischer arrived in London, accompanying American featherweight Jackie Wilson. When Fleischer saw the fresh-faced kid lined up as Wilson's opponent at the Blackfriars Ring, he was aghast. "The fight can't go on," he protested. "It would be manslaughter."

Wilson climbed through the ropes in a white silk dressing-gown emblazoned with the words "unofficial champion of the world" – he was to make it official in years to come – and leapt into the air with a nerve-tingling war-whoop. He then crossed to Ronnie's corner and whispered, "Don't worry, it won't be long now, son." The American's patronising attitude was misplaced. He was so exhausted at the final bell that he plummeted to the canvas as James was pulled off him. There was only one winner.

But James's long unbeaten run – more than 50 bouts – ended the same month. He dazzled Southern Area champion Dave Crowley for five rounds at the Wembley Arena, only for referee 'Pickles' Douglas, who had already warned the Welshman twice for low blows, to disqualify him in the sixth when he transgressed again.

The Swansea teenager was now moving in the topmost company and Spain's first world champion, bantam king Baltazar Sangchili, and an upholsterer from Gateshead, Billy Charlton, each outpointed him. But a second draw with East Ender Corbett revived his claims to title consideration. It would be a long time before they were fulfilled.

Frustration at his lack of recognition, worries over a damaged left hand, and impending marriage actually prompted James to announce his retirement – at 19! – and it was eight months before he regained his enthusiasm for the sport. Yet he still had 14 bouts in 1937 and 1938, his only reverses coming from foreign opposition: a surprise points loss to Dutchman Arnold Legrand and disqualification – once more for low blows – against the southpaw former world champion from Cincinnati, Freddie Miller.

This occasional carelessness to the body was to prove disastrous when Ronnie was finally granted a British title eliminator in April 1939. By now a lightweight, he was matched with former conqueror Crowley; history repeated itself, almost to the minute, and once again the sixth round saw James stray below the belt and find himself thrown out.

As Britain's boxers headed off for the big fight against Hitler, domestic concerns became secondary. But there was still room for annoyance at the generosity afforded to the champion, Eric Boon, managed by the influential Jack Solomons. Boon, having been called up, hid behind a Board of Control ruling that no titleholder should be compelled to defend his crown during the war: understandable if the fighter was serving abroad, but Eric remained in Britain.

James, on the other hand, did serve overseas and owes his safe return to Welsh light-heavy boss Glen Moody, who found him stranded at Dunkirk, without boots, his feet bleeding and swollen. Moody carried Ronnie (pack and all) on his back until he could transfer him to an Army lorry.

Granted ample leave to box as part of the Government's recognition of sport's importance to public morale, James kept on winning and new manager Billy 'Kid' Hughes, himself a veteran of more than 400 fights, kept his name in the headlines. Ronnie finally proved his superiority over Corbett – later killed in the Blitz – and forced Dave Crowley to retire after three painful rounds at Pontypridd. Yet it was not until August 12, 1944, that he was rewarded with that long-awaited title shot.

Boon had been invalided out of the RAF, apparently suffering from blackouts, and for a while his career was in doubt. But his main problem approaching the clash at Cardiff Arms Park lay in making the weight. The Welshman faced similar difficulties, but a fortnight's special leave and some hard work at his father's farm near Pontardawe enabled him to shed exactly a stone. Eric, however, needed two attempts before passing the scales. There can be little doubt that the effort to do so was responsible for one of the most one-sided championship contests in history.

Not that there were many complaints from the 35,000 who paid from five shillings to five guineas to see the first universally recognised British title fight in Wales. Ronnie performed superbly, relying on his boxing skills and refusing to be drawn into a slugging match, yet his punching power – particularly to the body – surprised the weight-weakened Boon. No fewer than 12 times the Englishman was floored, with the referee's count reaching

Ronnie watches Boon sign for their fight, with Bert James and Solomons

nine on six occasions. Only once was James in any difficulty, when Eric caught him momentarily off-guard with a right in the seventh round that briefly sent him to visit the canvas where the champion had spent so much of the evening. Ronnie soon resumed control, eventually bringing matters to a head in the 10th, when a left to the jaw, followed by a right to the body, ended Boon's hold on the crown. James's supporters, recognising his other talent, presented him with a piano.

The achievement of one ambition led to the pursuit of another: to bring back to Wales the world title once owned by Freddie Welsh. The lightweight scene was confused: the New York Commission recognised Bob Montgomery as champion, while the National Boxing Association, which covered most of the other states, preferred one Isaiah Williams, commonly known as 'Ike'. Perhaps it was the Welsh surname, but Williams was the man tempted to Cardiff to risk his share of the title against Ronnie.

Constant rain had left Ninian Park a quagmire, but the weather cleared for September 4, 1946, when 40,000 turned out to watch the first world title fight in Wales. But they and their hero seemed apprehensive in a quiet opening. The third round brought James's first success, an uppercut and three short lefts to the head, but Williams came back to score to the body. The fourth saw the first appearance of Ike's famous 'bolo punch', but James rode it well and edged the round. The 23-year-old American, despite a struggle to make the weight, stepped up the pace in the next two sessions.

Ronnie had the crowd on their feet with two solid blows to the champion's head at the start of the seventh, but the cheers were silenced when Ike dug a right hand deep into his rival's stomach, and the Welshman crumpled. He rose at nine, but needed all his courage and stamina to survive to the bell. Effectively, the contest was over.

The eighth saw the bolo in all its fearsome glory. A blow beneath the heart dropped James on to his knees, with his forehead on the canvas. Up at nine, an encore sent him down again for eight. A right to the head meant another count of nine, but Williams was unable to end it. Ronnie's bravery only meant further distress in the ninth. Three more times he was floored. Only twice did he beat the count. The slaughter was at an end.

The end is nigh – James falls before Ike Williams

His title ambitions were laid to rest, but James still needed money to look after his wife and five children. Within a fortnight of the Williams fight, he was arranging to go to Australia and meet local hero Vic Patrick, tempted by a guarantee of £25,000. But on the date set for the fight, Ronnie was nearly a stone over the agreed weight, and more than £10,000 had to be returned to aggrieved ticket-holders. The promoters insisted that he stayed in Sydney until the New Year and he duly beat welter champion Tommy Burns on a disqualification.

Ronnie and son Colin square up

Back home, the Board were pressing James to defend his domestic crown against Stan Hawthorne and he returned to Pontardawe determined to shed the surplus weight. But when Ronnie scaled nearly 9st 13lb for a warm-up at the Vetch against Swansea rival Cliff Curvis, there was no further reprieve. His title was taken away.

Inside the ropes, too, the younger Curvis proved too fast and too clever and the veteran's cornermen threw in the towel in the seventh. It signalled the end to a fine career.

There were brief thoughts of a comeback following a disastrous few months as a promoter, but they never came to fruition, and for a while he concentrated on management, steering Ammanford lightweight Reg Quinlan to a Welsh title in 1949. Two years later, Ronnie emigrated to Australia, feeling there was greater scope there for his (by now) seven children. He was a referee for 12 years, and worked as a masseur at the St George Rugby League club, one of his daughters marrying national captain Johnny Raper.

The chorister turned champion suffered a fatal heart attack while driving in Sydney in June 1977, at the age of 59.

COLIN JONES
(1959–   )

- **WBC Welterweight Challenger 1983**
- **WBA Welterweight Challenger 1985**
- **European Welterweight Champion 1982–1983**
- **Commonwealth Welterweight Champion 1981–1984**
- **British Welterweight Champion 1980–1982**
- **Olympic Representative 1976**

Kirkland Laing couldn't believe it. He had been giving this man a boxing lesson for eight rounds. Now, in the ninth, he was so much on top it was turning into an exhibition. He mixed audacious right leads with his left jabs, ripping in a bewildering succession of punches, and they were all getting through. But the blond figure in front of him was still walking forward, disdaining defence. And, frighteningly, he was laughing. The broad smile was briefly distorted as Laing's fist rapped home, but there was nothing Kirkland could do to remove it. And then it happened.

Colin Jones threw the left hook that was to win him the British title. Laing took it flush on the jaw, his gumshield flew over the heads of the startled ringsiders, and the champion grabbed at the top rope to keep from falling. The Welshman shoved him off, pummelling him around the ring before trapping him in the opposite corner. The punches rained in, and Laing was drained, physically and psychologically, when referee Roland Dakin called a halt.

"I knew I had him four or five seconds before I caught up with him," recalls Colin. "That's why I was laughing. I felt so good. I had the feeling I was going to nail him – Bang! Bang! It felt lovely!"

The sight of that blood-flecked grin, as much as any punch, destroyed Laing. For it indicated a man utterly certain of what was going to happen. And what's more, a man who enjoyed hitting people.

Mild-mannered outside the ropes, Jones became a tiger within. And it was a metamorphosis that began early. Born into a large family on a council estate at Gorseinon, just outside Swansea, Colin first pulled the gloves on just eight years later. His success was instant. There were a dozen Welsh age-group titles, with three British Schools championships to show his supremacy was not merely local.

His first season as a senior brought Welsh and British ABA honours, which clinched a trip to the Montreal Olympics. A few voices suggested he was too young at barely 17, but the apprentice electrician at Brynlliw Colliery was physically mature, already in the welter division he was to grace throughout his career.

The Games brought a unanimous points victory over Irishman Christy McLoughlin, followed by a similar defeat at the hands of lanky Romanian veteran Victor Zilberman, who went on to win

Colin Jones (right) and the 1976 Olympic squad

a bronze medal. They also provided a wealth of experience.

The pro vultures were circling, but wisdom prevailed and the Jones boy stayed another year among the Simon Pures, retaining his ABA crown and competing in the European Championships in East Germany. While there he lost his team tracksuit and the Welsh ABA sent him a bill for £40. Colin refused to pay it and turned pro with Eddie Thomas, making his bow at the Afan Lido in October 1977. Swansea boy Mike Copp put up stout opposition for four rounds, but tired and was floored by a right hand before referee Adrian Morgan shepherded him to safety in the fifth.

Ten more victories earned him an eliminator for the British welter title. The amazed audience at Caerphilly's Club Double Diamond saw Birmingham's Joey Mack down an incredible 10 times before referee Harry Gibbs decided

Colin with his mentor, Eddie Thomas

to end their final eliminator in the 10th round. Somehow Mack never seemed stunned, just unable to withstand the Welshman's left hooks.

A controversial knockout of the elusive Billy Waith – the result, the Cardiffian claimed, of kidney punches – paved the way for Colin to challenge holder Laing on April 1, 1980, at Wembley Conference Centre, where a large Welsh contingent watched the unbeaten Nottingham lad build up a massive points lead before the ninth-round demolition brought joy and jubilation to the singing Jones support, despair to the bemused ex-champion.

The first defence was as near to home as he could make it. The National Eisteddfod was held that year at nearby Gowerton, and three days after the festival ended the fight fraternity took over. The 'heddwch' ('peace') traditionally associated with the Eisteddfod Pavilion was replaced by 'war', with the champion putting his crown on the line against Abingdon's Peter Neal. The cultural atmosphere was maintained with pre-fight hymns from the Dowlais Male Choir, conducted by Wynford Jones, a man who, in his other guise (but the same suit), patrolled the rings as a referee.

Neal, a former Southern Area champion, quickly marked up and a cut along the eyebrow led Londoner Mike Jacobs, handling his first title fight, to halt matters midway through the fifth.

The European Boxing Union rejected calls for Colin to face their champion, Dane Jørgen Hansen, so the Welshman took out his annoyance on Guyana's Mark Harris in a scrap for the vacant Commonwealth belt in the familiar Wembley Conference Centre ring on March 3, 1981.

Harris had learned the game in New York, but although he proved to have all the moves, they contained more style than substance. Bruised knuckles on his right hand confined Jones almost entirely to the use of the left, but that was quite adequate for the job. A straight punch floored the Guyanese at the start of the second, and he paid further visits to the canvas in the sixth and twice in the ninth. Referee John Coyle, perhaps unnecessarily, allowed it to continue, but when a flurry to the head sent Harris crashing for the third time in the round he waved it off without a count.

The following month it was back to London to face Kirkland Laing once more, this time at the Albert Hall and with two titles at stake. In many ways, it was an action replay of their first meeting, but the recipe contained an added pinch of controversy.

As before, the Laing flair dominated the early stages, establishing a substantial lead, while Colin's patience would have made Job envious. However, the carefully laid plans so nearly went awry. In the eighth Laing abruptly switched his attack to the body and the champion went down clutching his foul-proof cup. Referee Coyle lectured Kirkland and gave Jones time to recover; as soon as hostilities resumed, Laing was on top of him, and a blow to the thigh sent Colin back to ground level. There was a lengthy pause with no count from Mr Coyle, and a collective holding of breath before Jones again pulled himself to his feet. Kirkland went into overdrive, chasing Colin around the ring, the shaken champion's composure and rhythm shattered. But just as defeat seemed imminent, Jones bounced off the ropes with a volley of left hooks which left Laing looking bewildered and frustrated.

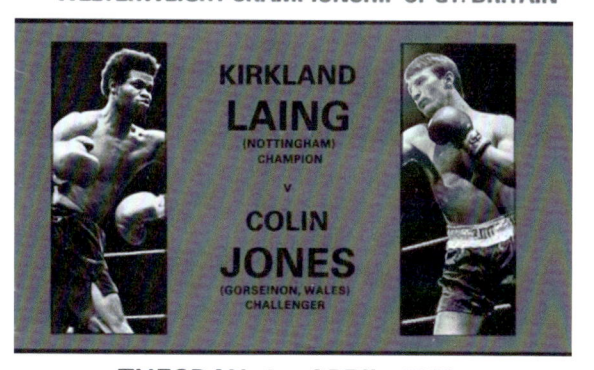

In the ninth the Welshman went after the challenger with the air of a schoolmaster bent on retribution. Lefts to the body showed Laing the folly of his earlier indiscretions, and he was already a picture of apprehension when Colin fired over a textbook left to the jaw – "probably the best punch

The Lonsdale Belt awaits

I ever threw" – and, although Kirkland marginally beat the count, Mr Coyle rightly rescued the uncoordinated figure before him.

But the smiles turned to tears next time out. It proved to be the last show held at Cardiff's Sophia Gardens Pavilion; the snows of the following winter brought down the roof, and the former aircraft hangar was demolished. For Colin, the roof fell in rather sooner. Curtis Ramsey, an import from Oregon, dropped to one knee under third-round pressure and, as he did so, was caught by a none-too-solid right to the head. Curtis hurled himself backwards as if shot, and referee Adrian Morgan, believing he had struck his head on the canvas and was too concussed to continue, disqualified the Welshman. Eddie Thomas was furious; Colin was inconsolable.

The next two American imports were despatched without problems and attention returned to Europe, and Hansen. The veteran preferred to hang up his gloves, and Jones was matched with the man all Denmark considered his logical successor, Hans-Henrik Palm. The bout was arranged for Copenhagen, but two hours before the weigh-in, Colin went down with appendicitis. While Jones was in a hospital bed, Palm stopped inept Frenchman Georges Warusfel in a hurriedly arranged match surprisingly accepted as worthy of the title.

Hans-Henrik was to prove a Palm from which it was unusually difficult to get a date. Jones saw off Fijian Sakaraia Ve in two rounds to keep his Commonwealth strap before finally flying to Copenhagen for his delayed chance on November 5, 1982. The fireworks flew in just one direction: Colin blasted straight through Hans-Henrik's guard and battered him to a stoppage loss inside two rounds, completing the title trinity achieved by manager Thomas at the same weight three decades earlier.

There was one goal still to be achieved, and the WBC duly matched Colin with the unbeaten Milton McCrory, a 21-year-old from the famous Kronk stable in Detroit, for their share of the title relinquished by the newly retired Sugar Ray Leonard. McCrory, a world junior champion, had a five-inch height advantage over the stocky Welshman, and his 20 straight wins saw him initially installed as a 6-1 favourite for their clash at Reno on March 19, 1983. A flood of Welsh money brought the odds down to 3-1 on the day of the fight, and Colin soon caused further revision by the worried bookmakers.

A right to the head in the second gave McCrory due warning of his power, and although the American kept scoring with the left jab, there was a broad smile on Jones's face at the end of the third. However, his certainty that he would eventually land the big one allowed Milton to pile up points while the Welshman bided his time. A left to the body in the sixth hurt McCrory, while blood began to seep from the American's nose in the next. The eighth saw another left to the stomach which sent the Kronk man on to his bike, to the crowd's displeasure, and a further body barrage in the ninth was followed by a one-two that buckled his legs.

The unattached support had now come down firmly behind Colin as he went looking for a finish in the 10th. But the fast McCrory left kept him at bay, and, almost incidentally, won him the round. The 11th was even, but in the 12th, screamed on by promoter Don King (who had now moved into the McCrory corner, any pretence of neutrality forgotten), the American finished strongly, Colin tending to pose rather than perform. The wait for the verdict seemed never-ending. Then came the heartbreaking news: Brazilian judge Newton Campos had voted 116-114 for Jones; José Juan Guerra, from Mexico, sided with McCrory, 116-113; and Venezuelan Dimas Fernández had it level 115-115. It was a draw.

Colin dumps Danish hero Hans-Henrik Palm

The anguish in each camp was at least eased by the prospect of a return, and the big pay cheques that would accompany it. In the event, Colin collected some $450,000 for his second crack at the crown, five months later, in a sun-scorched car park at the Dunes Hotel on the Las Vegas Strip. The temperature was touching 105 degrees as the pair climbed between the ropes at two in the afternoon, a time forced on them so that their conflict could be prime-time viewing in New York and Britain.

The temperatures of the travelling Welsh fans must have rocketed to a similar figure when their hero was put down in the first round. A left uppercut found its way between Jones's gloves, sending the Welshman to his knees against the ropes. Colin waited calmly for the count to reach eight before rising, the bell intervening as McCrory followed up. But manager Thomas later reckoned it took him three rounds to recover properly, and Milton again had an early lead.

Jones battled back bravely, and the fourth brought his first success with the left hook; McCrory blinked, and began to backpedal, the psychological balance of power beginning to tilt in the Welshman's favour. The left again rocked Milton in the fifth, and the following round saw blood flowing profusely from the Detroit man's nose. The seventh brought Colin to the brink of victory. A right over the jab, backed up by a left to the body, had McCrory in desperate flight, and it needed all his defensive ability to survive the round without going down.

The jubilant Jones support were to suffer a bewildering anti-climax. Colin, worried about punching himself out in the oven-like atmosphere, stood off and settled for a few jabs; McCrory, relieved, was able to regain his composure. Forced to cling on in the ninth, the American, as in Reno, dug deep and found enough reserves to stage a superb last-round effort as the two ignored the heat in a finale that had the fans in a ferment. Again, it had gone to the wire; again, there was the agonising wait for the decision.

Panamanian Angel Tovar favoured Jones 114–113, but Mexican Rey Solís made it 115–114 for his opponent. That left Venezuelan Anselmo Escobedo. And he scored it 115–111 – for McCrory. Again, the loss of the final round was decisive. Judge Solís had the two men even going into the 12th, which he gave to the American. The other way round and the split decision would have been in Colin's favour. Once more there were tears of frustration, coupled with the nagging thought that an all-out effort in the eighth might have made the judges' cards academic.

McCrory's handlers wanted no more of the Welshman, so world ambitions were redirected to the holder of the WBA version, an unbeaten Texan, Don Curry, also the inaugural champion of the newly formed IBF, though that body was unrecognized in Britain at the time. But there were out-of-ring problems to mar Colin's preparations.

The Board suspended his licence because of a defect in his left eye, only to restore it after specialists convinced them there had been no deterioration since he turned pro. And there was the worry of a long-delayed court case following a fracas outside a Gorseinon pub. Colin was acquitted of assault,

Colin Jones goes toe-to-toe with Milton McCrory

but the stress detracted from the concentration necessary for a major fight.

Curry, by anyone's judgment, merited total concentration. The 23-year-old 'Cobra', described by promoter Bob Arum as "technically the best fighter I've ever seen". This proved to be no hyperbole. There was class in every move the man made. This Curry was not merely hot stuff, he was vindaloo.

Colin waits as Don Curry moves in to attack ...

The size of Jones's task was soon made evident to the thousands who had sold out the National Exhibition Centre, near Birmingham, a month before the men came together on January 19, 1985. Three consecutive left jabs were thrust into the Welshman's face in the opening seconds, and any remaining doubts about his opponent's class were erased when Colin landed his favourite left hook to the body and Curry, far from flinching, responded with one of his own.

In the third the champion unleashed a left uppercut. It was merely a prelude to an onslaught of violent beauty, his hands weaving swift and repetitive patterns, with the Welshman the unmoving centre of a kaleidoscope of leather. When the show was over, so, effectively, was the contest. Curry stepped back to reveal a gaping wound across the bridge of Jones's prominent nose. Even the sound of the bell brought no relief.

There was nothing even such a consummate corner artist as Thomas

... and the aftermath

could do with such a gash. It needed barely a touch at the start of the fourth to bring the blood pouring down Colin's face. Puerto Rican referee 'Wiso' Fernández led the challenger to his corner, where a doctor made the obvious decision to stop the carnage. As Jones wept, resting his forehead against the top rope, a few bottles were thrown by those too far away or too drunk to appreciate the damage. Others, later revealed to be London gamblers rather than the Welsh fans originally blamed, attempted to storm the ring. It was an ugly and sad way to mark what proved to be the end of a great career.

For, despite a succession of proposed comebacks, Colin never did fight again. Repeated back pain ruled out a return and he turned to broadcasting work and, briefly, to management. He later began to train youngsters at his old Penyrheol club and was appointed national coach to the Welsh ABA in 2010, passing on the knowledge gained in a career that brought him three titles, even if he never quite scaled that ultimate pinnacle.

KEN JONES
(1949–   )

🥊 Welsh Light-Heavyweight Champion 1980

There is nothing like an enthusiastic and talented younger brother to motivate a man. Had it not been for the promise shown by his teenage sibling, Ken Jones might never have seen his name added to the scroll of Welsh pro champions.

He had already acquired a national amateur crown in the colours of Trostre ABC, winning at welterweight in 1968, but then married and drifted away from the game. But when Colin, almost 10 years younger, started to collect schoolboy honours, the eldest Jones boy was persuaded to return to the gym, this time at Penyrheol. In 1976, eight years after his first success, Ken added a second Welsh ABA championship, up at light-heavy, dispatching future promoter Colin Breen in the first of the final.

Colin, of course, went on to a British ABA triumph and the Montreal Olympics, but when he turned pro with the redoubtable Eddie Thomas in the autumn of 1977, Ken signed up too.

After four straight wins, including one over future British title challenger Trevor Cattouse, Ken suffered his first defeat. Guyana-born Londoner Dennis Andries had made his pro debut in Newport four months earlier, knocking out local boy Ray Pearce on the same bill that saw Jones outscore Cardiff rival Bonny McKenzie. On a dinner show in London's West End, Andries floored Ken in the first and won a six-round decision. No disgrace there – Dennis went on to have three spells as WBC light-heavy champion.

Despite that setback, Jones was given a shot at Welsh titleholder Chris Lawson on March 19, 1979.

Ken Jones gets revenge over Chris Lawson

The Cardigan man had the advantage of a West Wales venue, manager Eddie Thomas staging the bout before a 600-strong crowd at Haverfordwest's Market Hall. Ken was pushing forward, but the stylish Lawson kept him at bay with short jabs. The fifth saw Chris landing a right hook to the jaw that had the challenger looking anxiously to his corner as the crowd roared. By the seventh, Jones was bleeding from the nose and a cut over his left eye, but referee Jim Brimmell allowed him to carry on.

The Gorseinon man kept battling until the end, but Lawson – who had been married just two days earlier – was generally in control, winning by a two-round margin and free to set off on honeymoon without too many signs of his recent activity.

Jones travelled around Britain, claiming another decision over Cattouse along the way, before being given a second shot at Lawson and his belt. It came on August 12, 1980, a few miles from home at Gowerton in the Pavilion which had just hosted the National Eisteddfod. With kid brother Colin seeing off Swindon's Peter Neal to keep his British welter crown, Ken was able to make it a family double by gaining revenge over the classy Lawson.

Once again, Brimmell was the third man in the ring and this time he favoured Jones's high workrate and constant aggression over Chris's neat boxing and elusive movement. Toe-to-toe exchanges in the last session had the fans roaring, with the outcome in doubt until the final bell. Again there were two rounds between them, but this time Jones was out in front.

There was talk of a rubber match, but it never materialised. Ken boxed just once more, recovering from a slow start to draw with Londoner Steve Lewin in a "nobbings" fight at the Elephant and Castle. But the old enthusiasm was fading and marriage – his second of three – again took over his priorities.

Unlike Colin, Ken had no interest in becoming a trainer and has had little to do with the sport. Now retired from his factory job, he spends most of his time working on his smallholding.

RANDY JONES
(1911–1981)

Welsh Light-Heavyweight Champion 1933

By rights, Randolph Chelminsky Jones should never have been a boxer. When he was seven years old, at the end of World War I, he found a cartridge and, as boys do, began to play with it. Suddenly, it exploded, ripping off the index and middle fingers of his right hand. Whatever the youngster might go on to do for a living, a career in the ring seemed among the most improbable.

Yet the miner's son from Pontarddulais was not easily dissuaded. Packing his makeshift gloves with cloth to fill the gap where his fingers should be, he learned to look after himself. By the time he was 18 he was earning a few bob to supplement his wages as a labourer.

The Jones boy proved quite useful, too, with an early win over future Welsh middleweight challenger Trevor 'Tate' Evans and a series of close contests with the likes of Llanelli's Dai Watts and Wattie Phillips, from Llandybie. He held his own on a couple of trips to the West of England, while victories over Charlie Bundy and Big Jim Wilde underlined his progress at home.

There were also changes in his life, both private and professional. He married a Llanelli teenager, Hilda Cann, while forming another long-lasting partnership with Ammanford manager-promoter Johnny Vaughan. His new advisor's connections saw Randy entered for an open heavyweight tournament at Crystal Palace and he celebrated his London bow by halting Midlander Cyril Edwards, although his progress was ended in the next round by Seaman Atkey.

Randy Jones

If dreams of the big time in the big city had been dashed, things were looking up on the domestic scene, with another decision over the respected Bundy and success against Tonyrefail's useful George Smith – with whom he had drawn twice – brought a crack at the vacant Welsh light-heavyweight title.

In the opposite corner at Merthyr on March 11, 1933, was Jerry Daley, from Penygraig, who had dominated Wales's middleweights for two years before losing the crown to his predecessor, Glen Moody. Daley had acquired further experience as a sparring partner to both British heavy champion Jack Petersen and the man who would dethrone him later in the year, Len Harvey. No mug, then.

But he was labouring under a major disadvantage: he was conceding close to a stone in weight. And when he sustained a cut eye in the fourth round, his chances took a further blow. Jones was also the more skilful operator, his long left hand repeatedly finding the target, although he spoiled his performance with occasional wildness. Daley tried to nullify his physical limitations by focussing on the body, but Randy emerged a clear victor, prompting particular celebration as he became the fourth reigning Welsh champion from the Vaughan stable.

But there was another light-heavy attracting attention. Still only 20, though with more than six years as a pro, Tommy Farr had grown through the divisions and was now on the verge of a breakthrough at title level. The belt was not at stake when the Rhondda youngster faced Jones at Merthyr and the contest ended unsatisfactorily when Randy limped to his corner at the end of the sixth and announced that he could not continue. The consensus at ringside, however, was that Farr had been in control, his left lead scoring regularly, while his speed kept him away from Jones's counters.

A rematch for the championship was inevitable. It took place on the stage of Tonypandy's Empire Theatre on July 22, 1933, in a ring which had a slope of some two feet from one side to the other. But nothing disguised Farr's superiority and although the desperate holder rocked Tommy with a big right in the closing session it was far too late to affect the outcome. Wales's outstanding fighter of the inter-war years had claimed his first title.

Randy as an auxiliary fireman

For Farr, it was onwards and upwards. For Jones, there was little left. He began 1934 with a knockout loss at Crystal Palace thanks to a single right hook thrown by Teddy Phillips, one of a pair of Canadian brothers campaigning in Britain, and less than two weeks later – no compulsory suspensions in those days – he faced familiar foe Bundy at Swansea's Mannesmann Hall in a final eliminator for his old belt.

The stronger Bundy produced one of the best displays of his career, while Randy struggled to find any rhythm until the halfway mark. From then on, the former champion threw the more accurate punches and took the verdict and the right to seek revenge against Farr. That fight never happened. Jones was so dissatisfied with his effort that, following talks with manager Vaughan, he decided to hang up his gloves, just days after his 23rd birthday.

Randy and his family moved to Cardiff, where he lived in the Ely area and spent the war years working as a greaser on the city's buses. He still had an interest in boxing, however, and in 1946 opened a gym. But a few years later he upped sticks and headed for Western Australia, along with Hilda and their three children. Jones worked there as a guard at the mint and also trained would-be boxers at a local youth club. He died in Perth at the age of 70.

JOHN KAIGHIN
(1967–   )

🥊 Welsh Super-Middleweight Challenger 1993

Sometimes hard graft can bring surprising opportunities. But then you have to grasp them. The Swansea window-cleaner earned his chance, but then saw it slip away.

John Kaighin had no great boxing pedigree. Brecon-born, he lived for seven years in Liverpool, earning himself the nickname 'Scouse' when he settled in Swansea as a teenager. His only fisticuffs came when trouble broke out at the nightclub where he worked on the door.

But he showed one customer enough rough talent to impress. Former pro Mike Copp saw Kaighin go to work and suggested he should train properly. A few sessions in the gym at the rear of Copp's Sandfields house led to nine wins in 11 amateur bouts. Copp thought he should have another year in the vest, but John was 23 and impatient for a few bob in his pocket. After six defeats in his first seven, it looked as though his trainer had been right, but then Kaighin avenged a points loss to Llandovery's Robert Peel. Things began to change.

Sure, there were still plenty of losses on his record – including a rubber meeting with Peel – but they were matched by a few victories and the sort of draws in the other guy's backyard that amount to the same thing. There were occasional highlights, such as a one-round stoppage of former English ABA champion Keith Inglis.

But, generally, it was the life of the typical journeyman. On one occasion, John drove stablemate Mark Verikios to a show at Barking and discovered they were short of an opponent. "I borrowed Mark's kit and fought Peter Vosper to a draw," recalls Kaighin.

John Kaighin

A four-fight unbeaten run in the last three months of 1992, all across the border, earned John recognition from the Welsh Area Council, who had turned down a previously mooted Welsh title fight, but now paired him with a former conqueror, unbeaten Rhondda southpaw Darron Griffiths, to decide the first-ever champion at super-middleweight. A retirement loss to Norwegian prospect Ole Klemetsen – who had the legendary Emanuel Steward in the corner – made no difference and John climbed through the ropes at Cardiff's STAR Leisure Centre on March 24, 1993, with a belt in his sights.

He started confidently, targetting the body, but the 21-year-old Griffiths, moving up from middleweight, began to land in the second, prompting dismissive shakes of the head from the Swansea man, who then moved inside in a bid to rough up his more stylish rival. The tactic brought a lecture from Maesteg referee Mike Heatherwick, handling his first title bout.

By the fifth Kaighin's face was showing the effects of Darron's punches, but he was still competitive going into the sixth. Then a violent combination shook John to his boots and he was fortunate that Griffiths hesitated before following up. When he resumed his assault, however, there was no respite: with his back to the ropes, John scorned defence and tried to hit back, but four successive blows to the head convinced Mr Heatherwick that he had seen enough.

"I had a lot of support there, so I tried to impress them by dropping my hands. I stayed on the ropes too long and Darron caught me, but I still thought the ref was a bit premature," says Kaighin.

In the immediate disappointment, John announced his retirement, though he was back in the ring within five weeks. But after nine consecutive defeats – they came in good company, including Sammy Storey, Maurice Core, Noel Magee, Michael Gale and Garry Delaney – he suffered a broken jaw against Shaun Cummins, just as the area council decided to revoke his licence. It was restored on appeal and Kaighin reappeared after 20 months with a first-round knockout win.

But he had other priorities. Newly married and a father, he was also busy developing his new industrial cleaning business. After just two more contests in two years, John again hung up his gloves.

There was a flurry of activity on the unlicensed scene, with Kaighin winning a "Welsh championship" of sorts in his forties, before local gym-owner Chris Ware invited him to become a trainer. It worked out well: a couple of years later he guided his employer to the Welsh middleweight crown.

BARRIE KELLEY
(1972–   )

🥊 Welsh Super-Featherweight Champion 1993

Many future stars passed through the skilled hands of Trostre trainer Gareth Howells. And it was the legendary coach who unearthed a gem in Barrie Kelley, the middle of three sons (the youngest, Craig, also boxed) of Brian, a fitter at the works who later became the club's secretary.

Howells's efforts were soon rewarded with a clutch of age-group titles and a Gaelic Games gold medal, while Kelley's amateur career climaxed with a trip to the European Junior Championships and a controversial 3-2 defeat to Frenchman Julien Lorcy, later to become WBA lightweight king.

Barrie ignored the seniors to plump for an immediate switch to the pro ranks at 18, with Hywel Davies taking the managerial reins. Despite having to travel for much of his early action, the Llanelli lad lost just once – on cuts – in his first eight outings. Then, with an improvement in the standard of opposition, his fortunes changed.

A trip to Manchester saw him up against former Commonwealth challenger Michael Armstrong and, athough Barrie briefly dropped him in the opener, it was the Welshman who became intimately acquainted with the canvas, visiting it five times in all. Finally, cornerman Howells, whose jettisoned towel had been ignored by referee Ron Hackett, ordered his charge to stay down for the full count.

Next up was fellow-townsman Neil Haddock at Cardiff's historic Coal Exchange, the scene of the world's first million-pound deal in 1907. Haddock, like Armstrong a future British titleholder, also hit the deck in the opener, but rose to win a clear-cut points verdict. When three further defeats followed, all on the road, it was clearly time for a change. Out went Howells and Davies, to be replaced by Pat Thomas and former heavyweight Billy Aird, who was looking to promote in Cardiff.

Two wins suggested Barrie had made a wise decision and in his third engagement under his new team, at the Institute of Sport on January 19, 1993, found himself fighting for the Welsh super-feather belt. His preparations were not the best: a virus over Christmas saw his weight drop to 8st 2lb, but he was bang on the 9st 4lb limit when he faced North Walian Eddie Lloyd for the vacant title.

There was a further setback for Kelley in the second session when he injured his right hand, but he nevertheless dominated the early exchanges behind his jab. The vastly experienced Lloyd, who had contested the lightweight crown more than seven years previously, increased the pace in the middle rounds and Barrie was cut on the bridge of the nose, a wound expertly treated by Aird.

There was a further gash along his left eyebrow in the last, needing eight stitches, but Kelley was three rounds ahead on Roddy Evans's scorecard. Yet victory came at a price: while the facial damage soon healed, the hand was a different matter. He spent six weeks in plaster, followed by three months of physiotherapy and assorted injections to reduce the swelling, all to no avail. Experts then decided there must be a sliver of bone floating in the knuckle and booked him for surgery at West Wales General Hospital to remove it.

Barrie Kelley

It was nearly 10 months before Barrie returned to the ring, going straight into a defence of his title at Rhondda Leisure Centre against J.T. Williams, a hard-hitting former junior star from Cwmbran. Ironically, the problem hand functioned perfectly – it was another cut that cost Kelley his crown.

Williams's long left earned him the opener, but the champion responded with body shots to take the second. Then a clash of heads brought blood streaming from his left eyebrow and, although he survived a first corner inspection, the injury had deteriorated by the end of the third, prompting manager Aird to pull his man out.

Kelley's fragile features proved a continuing problem, a run of losses including two more on cuts, before a three-knockdown hammering by Cardiff traveller Tommy Janes prompted him to walk away from the game. The old urge was still there, however, and, after a three-year interval, he came back as a lightweight under the guidance of former trainer Thomas and Swansea-based Trevor Russell.

There were a few wins, but more losses and after being stopped by unbeaten Londoner Leo O'Reilly and reigning WBU king Colin Dunne, Barrie hung up the gloves for good.

Now living in his wife's home town, Ammanford, Kelley helped out at Hywel Davies's Towy gym for a while, but the pressure of work in a Llanelli bearings factory put an end to that.

JACK KILEY
(1917–1980)

Welsh Flyweight Champion 1938–39, 1940–46

The lad from Humphrey Street was still in his teens when he began adding to his income with a few judiciously placed punches. And he soon became a firm favourite with the punters who attended the rickety old Mannesmann Hall in the Plasmarl area of Swansea.

In fact, he rarely boxed anywhere else in his first few years as a pro. And it was, naturally, the venue for his first tilt at the Welsh flyweight title. Brecon's Dudley Lewis had only worn the crown for a couple of months, but making the weight was proving a problem and he relinquished in order to move up to bantam. On an unbeaten streak of 17 bouts, Kiley was a natural choice for one corner in the showdown to decide his successor; the other stool went to Rufus Enoch, one of a quartet of fighting brothers raised on a farm outside Tonyrefail.

Their meeting, on November 7, 1938, was interrupted after two rounds, when referee Ben Hardwicke spotted a flaw in the new gloves sported by Enoch. New mitts were brought to the ring, but these were also defective and a good five minutes had passed before a third pair passed the test and hostilities were resumed.

Then, within seconds, a barrage of straight lefts from Kiley opened a cut over Enoch's right eye. Rufus's two-fisted body assaults troubled Jack in the fourth, but his inability to see out of the damaged optic prevented him following up effectively. Despite desperate efforts between rounds, Enoch's seconds were unable to stem the bleeding and the towel that ended matters in the ninth was no surprise.

Having campaigned exclusively on Welsh soil, Jack finally ventured across Offa's Dyke to take on Joe Curran in the shadow of Blackpool Tower, but his habit of leaning forward as he moved in found him on the receiving end of a series of warnings. It was little surprise when Liverpudlian Curran, later to challenge Scot Jackie Paterson for the world title, had his arm raised. Kiley himself was to discover just how good Paterson was when he was tempted to face him in his Glasgow lair. The youngster, who succeeded fellow-countryman Benny Lynch on the British throne before the year was out, left-hooked Jack to defeat inside two minutes.

Jack Kiley's application for a Board licence

Kiley's first defence, against Markham's Ronnie Bishop – against whom he had already drawn and won – took place over the border at Gloucester's Kingsholm rugby ground on July 10, 1939. Jack was on top in the opener, but Bishop settled to launch a non-stop onslaught that continued until he was cut by a clash of heads in the fifth. The champion, encouraged, controlled the next few sessions, but Bishop, ignoring his lack of height and reach, waded into his man, pummelling him to the body and wearing him down sufficiently to earn Bob Hill's nod.

Kiley staked his claim for another title shot with what was lauded as the best performance of his career, flooring unbeaten fellow-townsman Willie Grey twice before the St Thomas man was pulled out with a damaged right hand, the injury that was eventually to bring a premature end to his career.

The rematch with Bishop came on May 13, 1940, with a Whit Monday crowd packing the Palace cinema in Crumlin for a fight which began at 7.15pm to allow workers to attend before going on night shift. They clocked in with heavy hearts, their man having been clearly outpointed. Ronnie deserved the applause he received for his gallant efforts, but his "hurricane tactics" never ruffled the challenger and the title went back to Swansea.

By this time Jack had joined the Monmouthshire Regiment, who were stationed in Northern Ireland in 1941, giving him the chance to outpoint local hero Bunty Doran, but boxing was very much on the back burner – especially as he was also newly married to Cynthia.

A cuts loss to Nantymoel rival Norman Lewis was his only serious ring activity in the next five years, with Kiley also needing time to recover from a broken leg – he had a steel plate inserted – which also ruled him out of front-line service. But when he was demobbed, rejoining long-time manager Sam Goldstone and resuming training at Port Tennant, he was still fit enough to box.

After reigning over Wales's flyweights for six years without defending, Jack felt he could no longer make eight stone and relinquished the belt. Ironically, two months later he was bang on that mark for his first postwar action, a points win over Brighton's Billy Hazelgrove. By then a series of eliminators was under way to decide his successor and Kiley found himself out in the cold.

There were only a couple more fights left. When double vision forced him to quit after one round against Abertridwr prospect Tommy Whittle it was enough for Jack, now 30, to call it a day.

He remained involved, however, running gyms at Landore, Penlan and Wind Street and playing his part in the careers of such as Alan Copp, Jeff Burns and Doug James. And all the time he could be forgiven for wondering what he might have achieved if the war had not stolen the best years of his career.

DEAN LYNCH
(1964–   )

🥊 Welsh Super-Featherweight Challenger 1989

Have gloves, will travel – that was Dean Lynch's motto. Only twice in a 20-fight pro career did he parade his skills before a Welsh audience. And his passport came in for regular use as he took on foes across Europe.

As an amateur with the Clase ABC, the boxing bricklayer had claimed a Welsh senior title before reaching the British final and losing inside the distance against future world title challenger Sean Murphy. There was international action, too, including success in a multi-nations tournament in Norway.

Dean was 21 when he signed up with manager Alan Davies, while David Roberts looked after the training side. The pattern was soon set: even though his debut opponent was a Welshman, Blaengarw boy Billy Barton, the bout still took place over the bridge in Weston. And Lynch lost the verdict.

But he won his next couple, including his first paid appearance in his homeland, when he took every round against Brummie journeyman Phil Lashley at the Patti Pavilion despite giving away almost a stone in weight. He repeated the feat when they met again in London and then claimed victory over one of the sport's legendary names. Unfortunately, this Henry Armstrong was not the three-weight world champion, but an optimistic Manchester lad really called Kevin Morris.

The reality of foreign trips as a boxer was brought home to Dean when he ventured to France to take on Raymond Armand. The local was already booked for a European super-feather challenge in Italy three weeks later, so even when his Welsh warm-up opponent floored him three times the judges still gave Armand the nod, thus keeping alive his important date. In fairness, Raymond took Sicilian Piero Morello to a majority decision in his home town, so perhaps he, too, suffered from a little "home cooking".

By now managed by Colin Breen, Dean, although naturally a featherweight, was called up to face

Dean Lynch

19-year-old exile James Hunter for the vacant Welsh belt up at 9st 4lb. They met on a John Davies-Teresa Breen co-promotion at Swansea Leisure Centre on April 12, 1989, and produced a thriller.

Lynch made a lightning-fast start and a right sent Hunter's mouthpiece sailing into the crowd. But James, based in Middlesbrough, but originally from Port Talbot, possessed the greater power and shook Dean with a right at the end of the first. The Swansea man, marking up under the left eye, tried to work his way inside, but Hunter's hands high, bob-and-weave stance made life difficult for him.

The third saw Lynch enjoy a little more success, but it was short-lived. The fourth saw James check his range with a left before exploding a right which sent Dean sprawling across the canvas, blood pouring from his cheek. He bravely hauled himself upright, but referee Wynford Jones would not let him continue.

From then on it was back to the travelling. Dean went to Italy to face Valerio Nati, who won a world title the same year, and Dominican Freddy Cruz, later to challenge WBO feather boss Steve Robinson. Both stopped him, but he did last the course with Dutch West Indian Regilio Tuur, who went on to capture the WBO super-feather strap.

Lynch took a couple of years out, but after half a dozen low-key contests with Mike Copp in the corner he called it a day for good. These days he and brother Paul – also a former pro, who once boxed Peter Manfredo, Sr, in the US – are the owners of a busy construction firm.

Dean is rescued against Hunter

ENZO MACCARINELLI
(1980–)

- **WBU Cruiserweight Champion 2003–06**
- **WBO Cruiserweight Champion 2006–08**
- **European Cruiserweight Champion 2010**
- **British Cruiserweight Champion 2012**
- **Commonwealth Light-Heavyweight Champion 2013–15**

Sometimes a boxer will have you leaping from your sofa, sometimes peering through your hands from behind it. Enzo Macc touched the two extremes more than most.

His punching power produced thrilling knockouts, but his own apparent vulnerability had his army of fans wincing. On several occasions, they pleaded with him to hang up the gloves; even his promoter, Frank Warren, went public with his wish that the amiable Swansea giant should call it a day.

The paradox was there from the start. When he made his first professional appearance on home soil, the programme was entitled 'From a Jack to a King'. He duly outpointed portly Midlander Nigel Rafferty – it was a tribute to Welsh choral tradition that, possibly for

Enzo Maccarinelli

the first and only time, *Who ate all the pies?* was sung in two-part harmony – and all seemed well, until he returned to Swansea Leisure Centre just three months later.

Manager Dai Gardiner had let his enthusiasm get the better of him, proclaiming that his 6ft 4in prodigy would become Wales's first world heavyweight champion. The suits at BBC Wales lapped it up and, for the first time for decades, decided to televise boxing live. Few 19-year-olds would have kept their focus in the face of such hype and after two comfortable rounds against Lincoln's useful Lee Swaby, Enzo went for a big finish to please the crowd; he walked straight on to a left hook and was still barely conscious when half-carried back to his stool.

It is to Maccarinelli's credit that the story did not end there. A lack of amateur experience – his Bonymaen club, run by Italian-born father Mario, was one of those rebelling against the Welsh ABA, denying him international opportunities – meant he needed to be brought along steadily. Belatedly realising that, his backers found him 10 successive victims and manoeuvred him into a position to challenge former British and Commonwealth king Bruce Scott for the vacant WBU cruiserweight crown.

With Frank Warren now in the promotional seat, the Welshman had home advantage on a Joe Calzaghe undercard at Cardiff International Arena on June 28, 2003. At 33, Scott had all the knowledge Enzo still lacked, but a snapped achilles had kept him sidelined for nearly two years. Not that any ringrust showed when he caught a nervous Maccarinelli with a sweeping left hook inside the first minute.

The Swansea man lurched back into the ropes and slid down before rising, still shaky, as referee Mickey Vann tolled a slow-seeming count. Enzo eventually complied with repeated requests to walk forward and the third man allowed him to continue. Somehow Scott was unable to find the finisher before the bell and, gradually, Maccarinelli began to settle. He hurt Bruce in the third, before a thunderous left hook late in the fourth spread the stocky Londoner beneath the ropes and Vann waved it off without counting.

An international selection of challengers came and went. Estonian Andrej Kiarsten and South African Earl Morais each lasted less than a round, while Essex hard man Garry Delaney was floored seven times and beaten in the eighth. Belgian survivor Ismail Abdoul's negativity enabled him to become the first to take Maccarinelli the distance, before Dane Jesper Kristiansen and American Richie LaMontagne were seen off in quick time.

A non-title trip to the Land of his Father saw Enzo despatch German Marco Heinichen in 98 seconds – missed by Mario, who was with grandson

Tobias Webb at the national boys' clubs semi-finals – while, in the main event, WBO boss Johnny Nelson edged out local Vincenzo Cantatore to safeguard a planned unification fight against the boy from Bonymaen.

It was duly set for the Calzaghe-Joe Lacy undercard in Manchester, but Nelson snapped knee tendons while sparring and Maccarinelli had to settle for another WBU defence, against Yorkshireman Mark Hobson, arranged at three weeks' notice. Under-motivated as a result of the switch, Enzo lacked composure, but a left-right combination in the third dropped Hobson and would decide the outcome after 12 tough rounds, in which the Welshman at times seemed intent on proving there was nothing wrong with his chin. Two judges favoured Enzo by a single point – thanks to that 10-8 third – in a hard-won unanimous verdict.

Enzo with beloved father Mario

With Nelson still sidelined, the WBO matched Maccarinelli with former WBC boss Marcelo Domínguez for the interim crown at the Millennium Stadium on July 6, 2006. The fight signalled a change in the Welsh corner. Veteran Cardiff trainer Charlie Pearson retired at 71, after six decades in the game, to spend more time with his wife. In his place came namesake Enzo Calzaghe, with big Enzo joining a thriving gym at the old Abercarn rugby clubhouse.

Domínguez, now 36, had never been stopped in a 15-year career, but there's a first time for everything! The Argentinian was dangerous early on, but his unsophisticated assaults took their toll on his stamina and by midway Maccarinelli could sense that the veteran was tiring. In the ninth a massive right sent Marcelo flying across the ring; although he managed to regain his feet, one look into glazed eyes convinced referee Paul Thomas to call a halt.

When Nelson finally admitted defeat in his battle for fitness, Enzo was automatically upgraded to full champion status. Once again Hobson, who had just picked up Enzo's discarded WBU belt, was drafted in to replace the stricken Sheffielder, vowing that this time things would be different. They were: one sweeping right caught Hobson behind the ear, flooring him and scrambling his nervous system to the extent that he staggered backwards as he rose and the contest was terminated after just 71 seconds.

Outclassed Canadian-American gipsy Bobby Gunn departed similarly quickly, while New Zealand-based Algerian Olympian Mohamed Azzaoui

Enzo in total control against Wayne Braithwaite

went in four. In between Maccarinelli needed the full course to outpoint former WBC champion Wayne 'Big Truck' Braithwaite, although he dominated throughout against the tough Guyanan. Unification beckoned. And that meant David Haye, who occupied the WBC and WBA thrones.

Their much anticipated showdown at London's impressive O2 Arena on March 8, 2008 – in truth, the small hours of the following day, to oblige US viewers – proved a disappointment and, for Enzo, a disaster. Personal problems had interfered with his preparation and a near-gallop to the ring hinted at his inner turmoil. Pre-fight punditry suggested that the Welshman should focus on surviving the early sessions and take over from a possibly weight-drained Haye late on.

But the Londoner had no such problems, underlining the fact by taking a drink before stepping on the scales. Nevertheless, Maccarinelli, ignoring Calzaghe's demand that he go all-out from the start, was fairly passive in a downbeat opener until a late blow which nicked Haye's left eyebrow. Trainer Adam Booth took a look in the interval and urged his man to "close the show".

He obeyed. A thunderous right had Maccarinelli sagging in a neutral corner, holding himself up by clinging to a rope. It merely meant Haye could continue his barrage, with Enzo defenceless to prevent the punches which finally dropped him. Instead of taking the eight-count to clear his head, the Welshman let pride take over and leapt to his feet too soon.

His wayward legs sent him lurching from one side of the ring to the other, before turning his back on referee John Keane and staggering into a post. The official looked into his eyes and, correctly, spread his arms to signal the end.

It began a series of painful defeats for Maccarinelli. Haye having moved up to heavyweight, Enzo faced London-born Ola Afolabi for the interim version of his old WBO crown and was knocked out in nine; unbeaten Russian southpaw Denis Lebedev needed just three rounds to acquire the vacant WBO Inter-Continental belt and calls for Enzo to pack it in became deafening, promoter Warren leading the way.

Maccarinelli saw things differently. A couple of one-round blow-outs of journeymen saw him head for St Petersburg and an under-the-radar tilt at the vacant European title on April 27, 2010, against local hero Alexander Kotlobay. The Russian, too, was wiped out inside a round and suddenly Enzo was back on track.

But his first defence, in Birmingham, against German-based Ukrainian Alexander Frenkel, revived fears among his fans that he might be seriously hurt. Comfortably in control, Enzo suddenly took a thunderous left hook in the seventh and went over; when he rose his eyes were elsewhere and his hands hung limply, but inept Finnish referee Erkki Meronen allowed Frenkel to land four more punches, leaving his defenceless victim flat on his back.

Thankfully, he soon recovered, but few expected him to box again. Indeed, he stayed away for a year before announcing that he was returning – at light-heavyweight. As a cruiser, the Swansea man had found himself in with naturally bigger opponents, but dropping to a division a whopping 25lb lighter was a huge gamble. He did so twice to halt journeymen, but then agreed to put the pounds back on and challenge British cruiser king Shane McPhilbin at Wolverhampton on March 23, 2012.

A chaotic opening round saw the crude Midlander drop Maccarinelli only for an incompetent timekeeper to sound the gong 47 seconds early. Enzo was decked again in the third, but recovered to floor McPhilbin in the ninth and take a clear unanimous decision. He never defended, preferring to drop back to the lighter class and tackle Commonwealth ruler Ovill McKenzie. That, too, was mired in controversy.

The big-hitting Jamaican had the challenger pinned to the ropes in the second and after a lengthy barrage referee Ian John-Lewis, clearly aware of Enzo's past history, jumped between them. The Welshman, who had successfully blocked most blows coming his way, was furious and John-

The night it all went wrong for Maccarinelli

Lewis tacitly admitted he had erred. A rematch was arranged for Cardiff's renamed Motorpoint Arena on August 17, 2013.

New trainer Gary Lockett, who had taken charge after the two Enzos fell out, was to play a major role in victory. Keeping a high guard and boxing well, Maccarinelli was growing in self-belief as he followed the plan to take the stamina-suspect McKenzie into the later rounds. But in the seventh he seemed to have reverted to the doubt-wracked figure who sleepwalked to defeat against Lebedev. Step up, Mr Lockett.

Gary let rip at his friend, finally asking what Mario, who had died the previous year, would be thinking of his son. It was the right button to press. Maccarinelli began to throw more punches, while Ovill's assaults lacked their earlier venom. Late in the 11th, the Derby man was exhausted and a powerful left uppercut had him out on his feet, sagging on to the ropes, face blank and hands by his hips. Enzo landed one more shot, high on

Enzo finishes Ovill McKenzie

McKenzie's bowed head, as referee Phil Edwards leapt to the rescue.

Within eight months, 'Big Macc' had the chance to become Wales's first two-weight world champion. It arose through a very 21st-century method of matchmaking. German promoters Sauerland Event tweeted that their champion, Jürgen Brähmer, would defend his WBA light-heavy belt at Rostock on April 5, 2014, with the opponent to be announced. Enzo saw this and responded: "Just checked my diary, guess what, I'm free that date! #havepassportwilltravel". The Welshman's supporters began to bombard the Sauerland brothers with support for the idea and within days the deal was done.

Maccarinelli drew first blood when Brähmer was cut by the right eye early in the opener, although replays confirmed it had been caused by a head clash. Yet that injury faded into insignificance when a solid left from the German in the closing exchange brought up a swelling which obscured Enzo's own right optic by the time he reached the stool.

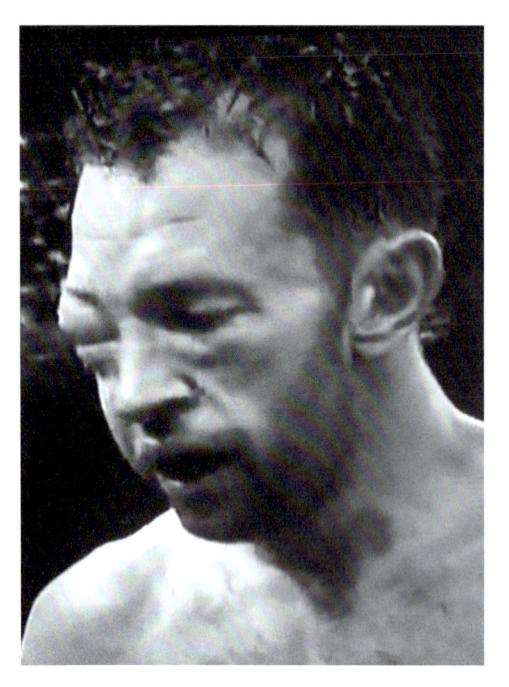

The damage that ended Enzo's shot at Jürgen Brähmer

At the end of the second he confessed to Lockett that he could see nothing, but told the doctor he had some vision. The medic allowed him to carry on and Gary, hoping his charge might land a fight-changing punch, let it pass. But Brähmer took the occasional left hook well and kept matters at close quarters, denying the challenger any leverage, and after the fifth the trainer signalled it was over.

Even then, the stubborn fighter wanted to continue. "I can't let you go on," Gary told him. "Look at your eye, Enz." "I can't see it," pointed out the Swansea man, with wry humour. But his brave adventure was over.

Maccarinelli campaigned for a rematch, but Brähmer defended against two other hopefuls before the year was out. Meanwhile, the Commonwealth Boxing Council ordered Enzo to put their belt on the line against British champion Bob Ajisafe, but the Welshman gave up the title to keep chasing his world dream.

MIGUEL MATTHEWS
(1965–   )

🥊 Welsh Super-Featherweight Challenger 1999

Most fighters who have reached a century of pro fights without a sniff of championship action would stop dreaming. But in the weird world of boxing the odd success can change everything. And when Miguel Matthews suddenly won bouts 104, 105 and 106, the Welsh Area Council were impressed.

They gave him the green light to face Merthyr's Chris Williams for the vacant Welsh super-feather title at Rhydycar Leisure Centre on September 24, 1999. The local boy was, naturally, the favourite. After all, he was a former amateur star with a cupboardful of silverware at home. But while Matthews was coming off a personal best treble, Williams had just been beaten in a round by future WBU lightweight king David Burke. If anyone was likely to feel the odd doubt, it was not going to be Miguel.

The name does not indicate any Spanish connection, despite manager Mac Williams's headline-hunting suggestion that he had been conceived when his parents were on holiday there during miners' fortnight. In fact, it was the age-old case of the father passing on his own name, but with a twist. Michael Matthews called his first-born, a girl, Michelle; when a son followed, he was christened Nicholas Miguel.

He had always wanted to box, but was unable to start until he was 21, when he bought his first car and could travel to the nearest boxing gym to his Ystalyfera home; it was the newly founded Blaenant ABC. He had only a dozen amateur contests – and his general fitness can be assumed from the fact that he boxed at light-middleweight.

Miguel Matthews

But he had slimmed down to featherweight by the time he signed up with Cardiff-based Williams, while former British title challenger Harry Carroll looked after the training side. A rift developed after a couple of years, with Matthews moving closer to home, both Mike Copp and Colin Breen becoming involved, but his role as a travelling "opponent" had already become established, with a plethora of future champions appearing on his dance card.

Colin McMillan, Naseem Hamed, Paul Ingle and Wales's own Barry Jones all went on to win world crowns, as did Dane Johnny Bredahl, whom Miguel floored, and Scott Harrison, whom he actually beat, albeit thanks to a cut eye.

The likes of Richie Wenton, Moussa Sangare, Paul Lloyd, Drew Docherty and Michael Brodie all challenged for the top prize. They, and many others on Matthews's CV, wore national and international belts. No wonder he was presented with the Board's special award for services to boxing. The man was hardly short of experience when he faced Williams and by now he also had former star Pat Cowdell to impart his wisdom in the corner.

The show was promoted by South African outfit Golden Fists, with Mbulelo Botile, the man who later dethroned IBF feather boss Ingle and left him fighting for his life, barely noticed on the undercard. The locals were there to see one of their own crowned as Welsh champion. They had their wish – but it was far from easy.

Williams used his southpaw leads to establish early command, with Miggy, perhaps hampered by ringrust for the first time in his life – 11 months had passed since his last action – taking time to get into the fight. His head-down style led inevitably to the odd collision, with Chris showing his annoyance and then responding with a deliberate butt, bringing both men a lecture from referee Roddy Evans.

The chants of "Olé, olé, olé!" from Miguel's followers seemed unusually appropriate and they had plenty of opportunities to give voice as their man came back to take the middle rounds. But another reckless charge saw Mr Evans deduct a point, with a warning that any further transgression could bring disqualification, and Williams kept on the move to take a 97-94 decision. Matthews was given generous applause as he left the ring, but his big chance had gone.

Three more contests – and three more points losses – saw Miguel end his career after 12 years and 110 bouts. The miner-turned-milkman-turned-coalman is now a builder and his connection with boxing is limited to training the odd white-collar enthusiast from his home village.

TERRY MATTHEWS
(1959–   )

🥊 Welsh Light-Middleweight Challenger 1981

The Swansea southpaw took a couple of enforcers into the ring. He called his right jab 'Ronnie' and his right hook 'Reggie' after the Krays.

A second cousin of the Curvis brothers, Terry began at 16 with the Gwent club, near his Townhill home, and soon won a Welsh intermediate title, beating best friend and future pro Jeff Aspell in the final. After just 19 amateur bouts, he made the switch with Colin Breen, while Jim Bromfield took care of the training.

In his paid debut in 1979 at Pontypool Leisure Centre, Matthews dropped a six-round decision to fellow first-timer Ronnie Pearce, though he still disputes it! He had 16 fights in two years before he appeared again in Wales – and it was against his debut opponent's brother.

Terry had won more than he lost on his travels across the border, although his best performance came as a late substitute in Manchester against unbeaten local prospect Wayne Barker, when he looked desperately unlucky to be given no more than a draw. But it would be fair to say he had not pulled up too many trees.

A sparmate of heavyweights Neville Meade and Winston Allen when at home, Matthews was called on as chief partner for world middleweight champion Alan Minter before he boxed Marvin Hagler and then helped Carlos Herrera prior to the Argentinian's shot at Maurice Hope's light-middle belt. Promoter Mickey Duff wanted him to move to London, suggesting he could earn good money by working with his top fighters or their imported rivals.

But Terry, with a wife and new baby, stayed at home and on April 7, 1981, at Newport nightclub Tiffany's, he faced Gary Pearce for the vacant Welsh light-middleweight title. Gary, the fifth of the six boxing sons of former booth fighter Wally, had tried for national honours at welter a year earlier but lost a close decision to another product of a pugilistic family, Horace McKenzie. This time he would get it right.

Matthews had barely trained, getting his fitness from a day job humping coal on to lorries at Swansea Docks, and there was a further blow when he came in nearly two pounds over the limit at the lunchtime weigh-in.

Terry Matthews (right) against Gary Pearce

He shed the surplus, thanks to 45 minutes' skipping in a sweatsuit loaned him by Pearce's heavyweight brother, David. Yet he was in control for the first couple of rounds, with Gary taking no risks as he contemplated the task.

Once the local man began to unleash, he tended to land, countering accurately as Terry tried to force the issue. A right uppercut in the fourth brought blood from the Swansea boxer's nose, but at the end of the following session Matthews turned on his stool to assure his ringside supporters that he was "still in with a chance".

It was a forlorn hope. Drained by the weight-making, Matthews was flagging and Pearce dominated the remainder of the action until top referee Jim Brimmell called it off late in the ninth.

Matthews regrouped, ending the year with quick victories over Midlander Neville Wilson and Rhondda boy Kenny Feahan and beginning 1982 in even more explosive form with a 45-second demolition of Pembroke's Steve Davies, but never had another opportunity at the Welsh title; ironically, Davies was to win it four years later.

When former stablemate Doug James won the vacant Welsh middle crown at the start of 1983, Terry optimistically challenged him, despite recent poor form, culminating in a cut-eye retirement loss to debut-making amateur sensation Errol Christie. To nobody's great surprise, it never happened. And Matthews never boxed again.

Along with cousin Keith Parry, Terry founded Montana ABC, but, disillusioned by a lack of interest, he left after two years and has had no involvement with the sport since.

FRANK McCORD
(1956–)

- **Welsh Welterweight Challenger 1982, 1983**
- **Welsh Light-Middleweight Challenger 1986**

Frank McCord's career was almost stifled at birth. He first attended the Gwent ABC gym as a 10-year-old, but when he arrived home late one evening, his father – also Frank – stopped him going. It was another seven years before the youngster from Cockett laced up a glove again.

After a brief amateur career under the guidance of Gwent guru Terry Grey, which brought him a Welsh international vest, McCord signed pro forms with Llanelli-based Glynne Davies. He later joined the ubiquitous Colin Breen, before finally managing himself, but trainer Jim Bromfield was a constant throughout.

Now living at Port Tennant and earning a crust as a bricklayer, McCord had a style which consisted largely of rumbling forward, clubbing away with both hands and hoping – often with good reason – that his foe would crumble under the constant pressure.

His sometimes rough-house methods brought retribution when referee Adrian Morgan turfed him out for using his head to work on a cut over the left eye of Llantwit Major's

Frank McCord on the pads with Jim Bromfield

Dil Collins. But he handed out punishment in more acceptable fashion to finish 1977 with two knockout wins. And he was a busy boy, boxing no fewer than 13 times the following year, ending the five-fight winning streak of Londoner Sid Smith and holding former British ABA champion Tommy Wright to a draw.

Future British light-welter challenger Steve Early flattened McCord in 99 seconds and, although there were sporadic successes, regular jobs as "the opponent" in the other man's backyard meant further additions to the loss column. But he was always operating at a decent level and the Welsh Area Council nominated him to face Cardiffian Billy Waith for the vacant national welter crown.

They came together at Swansea's Top Rank Suite on June 7, 1982, five years after Frank turned pro. Waith, a former British title challenger, had 87 fights behind him and had campaigned all around Europe; he was unlikely to worry about a trip 40 miles down the road.

McCord offered enthusiasm and fitness, but Billy had refined his craft and for the first three rounds demonstrated how he had come by the nickname of 'Will o' the Wisp'. His tattooed rival threw plenty of punches, but most struck the smoke-filled air or were blocked by the older man's arms. In the fourth, Waith began to land his left jab and it soon became clear even to those McCord fans in the back row that Billy believed in quality over quantity.

With Frank coming in with his head down, the Cardiff man began straightening him up with uppercuts and a five-shot combination had the local hero hanging on at the end of the sixth. McCord persisted in his brave march forwards, despite a cut right eye, but Billy's accuracy saw him through to a 99-97 margin on Jim Brimmell's card.

Frank was mixing in good company by now – although perhaps he could have done without meeting future world champion Lloyd Honeyghan, who despatched him inside a round – and soon found himself facing Waith for a second time, on December 12, 1983, again at the Top Rank.

There was a decent turnout as promoter Alan Davies experimented with a Saturday afternoon show and most were supporting McCord. Waith was gashed over the left eye in the opening session, but the 33-year-old soon took command of the ring centre. His jabs and occasional hooks to the body took their toll, with Frank forced to hold at the end of the seventh and eighth. There was little complaint when referee Ivor Bassett had Billy three rounds up at the end.

McCord had only five outings in more than two years before an unexpected third chance of Welsh title glory, at Swansea Leisure Centre on March 26,

1986, when he was hastily matched with Pembroke southpaw Steve Davies in a replacement main event for the vacant light-middle honour.

As well as his wrong-way-round stance, Davies had height, reach and weight on his side and soon capitalised on those advantages. Frank needed to work his way inside, but each time walked on to Steve's right hook. Hurt in the opener, he battled back, but was taking more than he threw and in the fourth a toe-to-toe exchange saw him come off second, stumbling forward to the canvas.

Up too soon at three, Frank immediately found himself on the deck again, this time striking the back of his head on the bottom rope as he fell. He dug deep and dragged himself upright, but was clearly still shaky and the referee waved it off.

It was time for a change of scenery. Frank bought a bar in Marbella, but reappeared in the ring after coming home for the winter. A sixth-round stoppage by unbeaten Midlander Kevin Thompson in Cardiff convinced him it was time to finish.

He stayed on the Costa del Sol for another eight years, before renting the bar out and returning to Swansea to run a building and roofing company. He trained son Ross throughout the boy's career, but is no longer involved in the sport.

ROSS McCORD
(1977–   )

Welsh Welterweight Challenger 2002

It was all set up to be the highlight of the young man's career. He was going to succeed where father Frank had failed three times and become a Welsh champion. The old man even invested in a special belt to be presented at the end, given that the cash-strapped Welsh Area Council were unable to provide one.

Few of those who left their Sunday lunch to pack the Swansea Leisure Centre on September 15, 2002, anticipated much from the other horse in the race. After all, Keith Jones, a 33-year-old factory worker, was the archetypal journeyman; he had only seven victories from 77 fights and had not won for more than two years.

But there is a world of difference between rolling up at short notice to go through the motions against a hometown prospect and being given the opportunity to contest your national championship. Jones was well prepared, focussed and confident.

The Cefn Hengoed southpaw had gone the distance with Jason Cook in a previous Welsh title tilt and crossed gloves with other belt-wearers, including Dean Pithie, Roy Rutherford, Ted Bami and Alex Moon. There was nobody on McCord's roster to match those names and the experience fighting them must bring.

Facing his first 10-rounder, Ross planned to take things steadily at the start, working behind the jab before picking up the pace in the later rounds. But those rounds never came. Jones stormed out from the off, disconcerting McCord and amazing those used to watching him in survival mode. Brushing aside Ross's tentative left leads, Keith poured on the

Ross McCord

pressure, targeting the body. His eagerness even led to a left hook landing after the bell, although his instant apology was sportingly accepted by the recipient.

The underdog was equally aggressive in the second, even leading with right hooks on occasion and forcing McCord to the ropes. The local slid to the canvas early in the third, but referee Roddy Evans lectured Jones for a low blow. There were no doubts about the punch that decked Ross late in the session.

And although the bell came to his rescue then, there was almost a minute left in the fourth when Mr Evans called a halt after Keith had dropped him with a succession of right uppercuts. The stunned audience pulled themselves together in time to join the McCord camp in applauding the unexpected champion.

For Ross, it was a shattering defeat which drained him of any desire to return to the ring, ending a career which had seen its successes, too. Beginning as a nine-year-old, he belonged to a fair number of Swansea's amateur clubs, reaching a series of national finals, but winning just one schoolboy title.

McCord turned pro at 20 with his father's manager, Glynne Davies, although he switched after a year to Colin Breen and, in due course, to Paul Boyce. With Dad and Jim Bromfield training him, Ross recovered from a debut cuts loss to stop his next two foes, but tended to come second on his trips across the border.

At home, where his popularity was reflected in the ticket sales, he was more successful, although twice dropping highly contentious decisions to Gelligaer trier Woody Greenway. Ross enjoyed a little luck himself when he was handed a draw against Marcus Portman, later to challenge for both British and Commonwealth crowns.

Following the Jones disaster, he walked away from boxing, returning briefly to train long-time friend Darryn Bushbye and fellow Swansea fighter Greg Pickin, but they had only a handful of appearances before work prompted them to give up the ring. Since then Ross has focussed on the family building firm he now runs.

NEVILLE MEADE
(1947–2010)

- **British Heavyweight Champion 1981–1983**
- **Commonwealth Games Gold Medallist 1974**

Thirty days after his 34th birthday, Neville Meade wrote his name into history. At an age when most fighters are settling into more peaceful lifestyles, the big man from Swansea became the oldest heavyweight champion Britain had known. The 'Cinderella Man' of Welsh boxing had reached the ball just in time.

The route was long and winding, beginning in Jamaica. Neville's parents migrated to Britain in the 1950s, leaving the youngster in the care of his grandmother. Neville rejoined his mother and father when he was 10, in Ipswich, where he first laced on the gloves at Lancer Secondary Modern School after demonstrating his power in unconventional fashion.

A PE teacher, proud of his stomach muscles, used to challenge his pupils to test them with a punch. "When he picked me, I walloped him," recalled Neville. "He threw his potatoes all over the place!"

Boxing, however, was a poor third to cricket and athletics, and remained an occasional activity even after he had signed up for a nine-year term in the RAF. But the sight of a hulking young airman soon attracted the attention of the men in charge of the boxing team. Cpl. Meade went on to win four RAF heavyweight titles, three times adding the Combined

Neville Meade

Services crown and reaching the British ABA final in 1973. He was outpointed by Garfield McEwan, but the Brummie dropped to light-heavy and Meade took his place in the England Commonwealth Games team for Christchurch the following January. Men from Canada, Western Samoa and Nigeria were swept aside, and the 26-year-old was garlanded with the gold medal.

Neville rounded off his amateur success by capturing the ABA crown that had eluded him, and pro managers were hovering. Somewhat surprisingly, he signed for Glynne Davies, a 31-year-old former bantamweight from Llanelli. His wife and children were already in Wales, and, on leaving the service, he moved to Swansea.

His debut was less than sensational. Referee Doug Jenkins considered, virtually alone among those at the World Sporting Club, that Meade had lost to the unbeaten Toni Mikulski, from Portsmouth. But the following month saw victory in a £2,000 open heavyweight competition at the same venue, Neville's first two foes knocked out in a combined total of 67 seconds.

It was no golden ticket. Retirement losses to Richard Dunn, on his way to British, European and Commonwealth titles and a brave challenge to Muhammad Ali, and fellow-Jamaican Tony Moore bruised his self-belief, while manager Davies opted to revive his own boxing career and passed him on to businessman Eddie Richards.

New trainers Cliff Curvis and Dickie Dobbs went to work. While Curvis honed his skills, Dobbs had the big man running up and down the dunes to build up strength. The results were immediate. He drew and won against former conqueror Moore in a streak that concluded in Paris with a three-round stoppage of unbeaten French prospect Lucien Rodriguez, later to win the European title. Another future continental king, Alfredo Evangelista, outscored Neville in Madrid, but the Swansea man was soon to be a champion himself.

At the Top Rank in his adopted home on March 29, 1976, Meade blasted aside Tonyrefail youngster Tony Blackburn in four to collect the vacant Welsh crown. British honours were now in his sights, but in the sweltering heat of Sophia Gardens Pavilion, Neville was halted in seven rounds of an eliminator by former amateur victim Denton Ruddock, a disaster followed by an early defeat against unbeaten Londoner John L. Gardner.

Neville broadened his horizons, fighting in Norway, Belgium and South Africa, but, with training now something of a chore – and one with which he rarely troubled himself – there were three successive stoppage losses before the bout that turned his career around. David Pearce, a 20-year-old from Newport, had won his first nine as a pro, climaxed by a quick win over Ruddock. Taking the Welsh title off an unenthusiastic champion was seen as the next step, but Meade, at a heaviest-ever 17st, dwarfed the apprehensive challenger and battered him to defeat inside two rounds.

"I'd been going through the motions," he acknowledged. "But that win made me realise I still had something to offer."

Another Welsh prospect, Cardiff's Winston Allen, also fell in the second after a nerve-jangling delay when Neville's massive fists proved too big for the gloves provided. Back in British title contention, this time he did not muff the opportunity. But it needed all Neville's new-found determination to take him past the first obstacle, lanky Londoner Stan McDermott, in a wild brawl that looked as if it had been choreographed for a low-budget Western. Floored in the fourth, Meade rose to win it in the fifth and his next hurdle was easier: Leeds West Indian Terry Mintus, only seven months younger than Neville, was swept aside in three rounds at Ebbw Vale Leisure Centre.

It set up a shot at the new owner of the Lonsdale Belt, Ulsterman Gordon Ferris, at the Aston Villa Leisure Centre on October 12, 1981. The pair made a stark contrast: the dark Meade, balding, paunchy, and weighing 16st 3lb, Ferris, tattoos stark against his pale skin, looking sharp and athletic at 14st 8 1/2lb.

The locally based holder, an overwhelming favourite, was soon landing his jab, his rival unable to land a glove on him. A one-sided opener was drawing to a close when it happened. At last the challenger scored with a straight left. As ever, it was the rangefinder for the right. Over it came, the punch Neville called "Baby Grand", thudding into the side of Ferris's head. He crashed on to his stomach, his face pressing into the canvas as Mike Jacobs counted him out. Britain had a new heavyweight champion, the oldest ever, and it had taken just two minutes and 45 seconds.

The new monarch, who had been handling his own affairs since leaving Richards, promptly signed with the influential Terry Lawless, but looked awful in losing

Neville flattens Stan McDermott

a 10-rounder against shaven-headed American Leroy Boone. Then he knocked out another Yank, tubby novice Ricky Kellar, but did not impress. It would be 19 months before he climbed into a ring again.

Promoters were not rushing to his door, with heavyweight attention focused on Frank Bruno, who apparently had no time for the once coveted championship. Young Pearce had fought his way back into the frame, but his handlers raised a string of objections over dates and venues. And when this was all sorted out, Meade injured an elbow.

The two Welshmen finally came together at Cardiff's palatial new St David's Hall on September 30, 1983. It was the last British championship fight to be scheduled for 15 rounds, but few thought Meade likely to last that long – win or lose. In the event, his fitness surprised many, and at 15st 6 1/2lb he was only a stone heavier than the challenger. He stood immobile, with a wry smile, as the psyched-up Pearce bounded about the ring during the preliminaries, but beneath the Newport man's excitement was a greater maturity than three years earlier.

Neville concentrated on the left jab, mostly absorbed into Pearce's high-held gloves, but occasionally jolting through. And he ended the second with a volley of right uppercuts and left crosses which, ironically, provided David the reassurance he needed: this time he could withstand Meade's blows. The champion was moving ahead, but with a points decision always improbable this was largely academic. Even a solid uppercut in the fourth brought only a grin from the bearded Pearce, and the Swansea contingent's noisy support began to decrease in volume. The challenger's growing

Neville Meade with (from left) Colin Breen, Alan and Michael Copp, Eddie Richards, Cliff Curvis and Dickie Dobbs

confidence was reflected when he pushed the heavier man back across the ring; it was time to go on the offensive.

The gear-change was gradual. There was no wild assault, but the toe-to-toe confrontation became more even-handed, with Pearce turning his attention to the head as the 36-year-old champion's hands began to drop. The seventh found Meade trapped in his opponent's corner, looking weary as David pounded him, but the cautious challenger let him off the hook. When Neville landed a thunderous left to Pearce's jaw midway through the eighth, he must have felt he had again pulled off the impossible; when David merely turned to the Swansea fans and laughed, Meade knew it was all over. He stepped back, slipped on water in his corner and Pearce leapt in with a quick right to drop him on to one knee. As Neville took a nine-second rest, he looked as old as Methuselah.

He survived the round and found the energy for one last, despairing flurry in the ninth. Pearce bided his time, and when the attack was spent, produced a perfect left hook which left his man sagging against the ropes. Referee Roland Dakin responded instantly, holding back David's follow-up right and signalling that the exhausted Meade was a champion no more.

In retirement the big man stumbled into the clutches of alcoholism and at one time was living on the streets. Just as things began to improve, he was diagnosed with cancer and died, aged 61, in the Tŷ Olwen hospice at Morriston Hospital.

Neville Meade may not have been an outstanding champion, but he always conducted himself with dignity and his perseverance stands as a lesson to many with greater talent.

DAMIAN OWEN
(1985–)

🥊 Welsh Lightweight Champion 2007–2011

Scientists say much of our behaviour is conditioned by our environment. That being the case, it was always pretty likely that the Swansea boy would take to the ring.

Damian Owen was the fourth of seven brothers; while the eldest never boxed, the rest all climbed through the ropes when in their teens.

Apart from Leon, who won national honours at junior and senior level and had half a dozen pro fights, Damian – known to all and sundry as 'Donk' – was the only one to continue into adulthood. After a decent, but unexceptional amateur career with Portmead and Blaenymaes, he switched over at 19 with Aberystwyth-based manager Nick Hodges. Nearer to home, Paul Grenfell looked after the training side.

Owen began with two stoppages in three straight wins – Birkenhead's Peter Allen lasted just 18 seconds – and was then matched with Polish Olympian Dariusz Snarski, a European title challenger in the paid ranks, in a scrap that would have told the Welshman where he stood in the game. Alas, Snarski pulled out and Damian had to settle for a routine points success over London-South African Bheki Moyo.

The question of status was answered next time out, however, when Owen travelled to Ulster to take on Commonwealth Games rep Kevin O'Hara, who had just been outpointed in a Celtic super-feather challenge to Willie Limond in Glasgow. On the first pro show at Lurgan for half a century, O'Hara kept the locals happy with a two-point victory.

Damian Owen with daughter Abigail

But Damian was not prepared to accept his place in the pecking order. He saw off ringwise Midlander Carl Allen before showing Northern Ireland fans the real 'Donk' by climbing off the deck to stop Scouser Stephen Mullin. A first appearance on home soil saw a points triumph over Belarussian Yevgeni Kruglik and set him up for a shot at the Welsh lightweight crown, uncontested for nearly 12 years.

'Donk' moves in on Dean Phillips

He was matched with Llanelli veteran Dean Phillips on the undercard of the Scott Gammer-Danny Williams British heavyweight title fight on March 2, 2007, at Neath Sports Centre, and his 10-year advantage over the 31-year-old computer programmer proved decisive.

Not only was youthful speed and mobility vital in helping Owen establish the early pace, Phillips's ageing body decided to rebel, damage to his left shoulder leaving him unable to deploy his main weapon. Damian's aggressive opening had already laid down a marker, however, even if an early shot from Dean had left a red blotch on Owen's prominent cheekbone.

When a solid right turned Phillips's head on its axis, Owen's fans set up a jubilant chant of 'Donk-o!'. But it was when their favourite turned his attention to the body that the belt came his way. A corkscrew left down below sent Dean to a squatting position, his face distorted with pain, and he stayed there throughout referee Wynford Jones's count.

With Tommy Gilmour now in the manager's seat, Owen headed for Motherwell as part of the Scot's plans to build his profile. But nobody had told Pedro Verdú, the Catalan-based Venezuelan hired for the opposite stool. Verdú had not won for three years, but found Damian easy to reach with long rights. One such, in the third, saw him stumble to the canvas and he was still unsteady on rising, prompting referee Paul Graham to jump to the rescue as the South American stormed in.

Owen responded by taking every round over Wiltshire trier Chris Long at the Brangwyn Hall – Damian's only outing in his native city – but injuries and extra-curricular distractions meant he boxed only three more times in four years.

There were a couple of wins and, after a long lay-off, he took future British and Commonwealth title challenger Tyrone Nurse to a single point before his Huddersfield faithful.

Since then there have been sporadic rumours of a return, but, now past 30, it seems unlikely we will see him climb through the ropes again.

KEITH PARRY
(1963–)

Welsh Lightweight Champion 1987–89

When Swansea boy Keith Parry made his pro debut at Blaenavon Leisure Centre in the autumn of 1985, Andrew Williams was topping the bill. But, despite the gulf between them at the time, people were already talking about a collision down the road.

Parry – kid brothers Carl and Paul also boxed, actually starting before Keith – had beaten Williams on an amateur club show and a rematch in the paid ranks seemed inevitable. Six straight wins gave the Townhill youngster a great start to his new career and earned him the fight he wanted. Williams had just won the vacant Welsh lightweight crown and was seeking his first challenger. The hard-hitting Parry, who had halted his last four foes, was an obvious choice and they met at Ebbw Vale Leisure Centre on July 30, 1986.

Keith suffered his first defeat, yet he came within seconds of victory in a thriller that lived up to the tradition of tremendous battles for the Welsh 9st 9lb crown. Facing his first lefty as a pro, the challenger seemed confused at first, while Williams, still only 20 and two years younger than his long-haired opponent, commanded the ring and even dropped his man

Keith Parry celebrates

with a chopping right early in the third. While Andy lacked power and was unable to close the show, there was no shortage of venom in Parry's punches, and the fight's intensity led the pair to continue their argument past the bell to end the sixth, prompting some stern finger-wagging from referee Adrian Morgan.

Williams seemed comfortably in control, but a left hook midway through the eighth sent him sliding down the ropes to the canvas. He rose at seven, but was again under pressure at the end of the round. Keith stormed out for the ninth, and a corkscrew left to the body stretched the Garndiffaith man near his own corner. He struggled to clamber up at five, but Mr Morgan, after a long look, let him continue. Somehow Andy stayed clear of that lethal left for the remaining minutes and held on to his title by a three-round margin. Everyone present knew the duo would have to meet again, yet it took more than a year to happen.

Williams had already agreed to face Mervyn Bennett next, so hiring Parry for the Cardiffian's warm-up was less than sensible: Keith duly shattered Mervyn's plans (and those of promoter Heddwyn Taylor) by halting him in three rounds. He continued to dispose of potential rivals, outpointing Rhyl donkey man Eddie Lloyd in Cardiff, but then had a reality check in a non-title points defeat by British champion Tony Willis at St David's Hall. The Brummie southpaw finished three points up; the gap was wider when Parry travelled to South Africa to face Elijah Cele.

Finally, Keith was given his second chance at Williams, at the Mayfair Suite in his home city on October 28, 1987, the day after his 24th birthday. This time he had few problems with Andy's wrong-way-round stance and in the second a right to the holder's jaw sent him crashing on his back. But Williams began to take control with his neat boxing, a frustrated Parry tossing a desperate right after the gong to earn a lecture from the referee, again Adrian Morgan. This time, however, the challenger was willing to take a few to get inside and he took over in the middle rounds.

Andy briefly visited the canvas early in the eighth – it looked a slip – but there was no doubt about the next knockdown. Parry forced him into a neutral corner and unleashed a chilling left to the jaw; Williams revolved on his heels before sprawling beneath the bottom rope and almost rolling on to the ringside press table. He hauled himself up at eight, but Mr Morgan had seen enough. Wales had a new lightweight king.

Parry was paired with Chorley's Carl Crook in a British title eliminator on April 26, 1988, at Bradford's St George's Hall, but once-beaten Crook's ringcraft and accuracy kept Keith at bay, with the visitor cut near the left eye from early on. Referee Mickey Vann had five rounds between them at the end.

The final curtain was near. Before Keith faced London-based Ugandan Patrick Kamy in Evesham his preparation was disrupted when trainer Jim Bromfield split with manager Colin Breen. He went through with the engagement and it proved a proper tear-up: the African was floored in the first and third, but landed a big right hand in the sixth which sent the Welshman to the deck in slow motion. Although he managed to continue, he had little left and referee Paul Thomas came to the rescue.

Parry called it a day, but when Bromfield returned to the gym some months later he changed his mind. Then, when it came to renewing his licence, he failed the Board's brain scan. Just 26, his career was over.

Disillusioned, he walked away from the game, but he has now yielded to the old passion. For the past nine years Keith has assisted former amateur coach Terry Grey in bringing through the next generation at Gwent ABC.

GEOFF PEGLER
(1959–)

- **Welsh Light-Welterweight Champion 1983–84**
- **Welsh Welterweight Champion 1986**

Cross-city rivalries are a great thing in boxing. But sometimes they can get a bit out of hand. And that tended to happen when Geoff Pegler came face to face with Ray Price, at least after 'Sugar' Ray had been awarded a tight decision and the Welsh light-welter crown when they first met in the ring.

The fact that Geoff was courting Ray's cousin – now his wife of more than 30 years – added to the mix. There were plenty of unscheduled rematches on the streets of Swansea before they came together officially with the title again at stake. It was to go down as a black night in Welsh boxing history.

Soldier-turned-scaffolder Geoff was a useful amateur with the Swansea Docks club and reached the senior Welsh ABA final in 1980, losing to Newport southpaw Paul Lewis, before turning pro with Colin Breen. Life in the paid ranks started with a points defeat, but the Port Tennant man lost only once in his next eight contests, and that by half a point against future British welter king Kostas Petrou. That form earned him a shot at the vacant Welsh light-welter title – and that man Price, a former stablemate now in dispute with Breen, was selected for the other corner at the Top Rank Suite on March 22, 1982.

Geoff was the early aggressor, paying determined attention to his foe's midriff. But Price's clever boxing gradually saw him taking control as he began to find the range with his southpaw jab. Pegler staggered his man in the last, but it was too late and Wales's top referee, Jim Brimmell, raised Ray's arm at the end of a thriller.

By the time they met again, on May 27, 1983, the personal animosity was at its height. Some 30 drunken youngsters had left the Top Rank balcony to move into the ringside seats, where scuffles broke out. Beer was thrown over a Pegler supporter, whose companions retaliated by hurling empty glasses at those fans remaining upstairs; their targets responded by throwing chairs into the hall. As the boxers were rushed back to the dressing-rooms, an all-out brawl broke out, involving at least 100 people. Unfortunately, the men being paid to fight were no longer able to do so.

It took seven months to organise a third clash, at Swansea's Dolphin Hotel on December 19, 1983. At first Ray's left was constantly in Geoff's face, while his mobility kept him clear of retaliation. But in the fourth Pegler landed a left downstairs that had a noticeable effect and, although Price battled back, it was a sign that the tide was turning. The holder found himself in more trouble when a clash of heads left him bleeding from a gash by his right eye. Although it survived a corner inspection, another collision made the problem worse. The Price camp had little option but to retire their man at the round's end.

Geoff Pegler signs with Colin Breen

The new champion was never to defend; indeed, Pegler never again boxed at light-welterweight. But there was one night of glory still to come.

Two years earlier, a young man of Italian extraction, Rocky Feliciello, had halted Swansea's John McGlynn to win the vacant Welsh light-middle crown. But on March 14, 1986, it was at welter that the Rhyl boxer, to the cheers of his home fans at the Ffordd Las Social Club, faced Pegler, four years older, to dispute the empty national throne.

The local's day began badly when he was a pound and a half overweight. Yet he set a hot pace, jabbing and hooking, while Pegler's success was limited to one solid left to the body, immediately cancelled out by a crisp right counter. But a cut left eyebrow dented Feliciello's early self-belief and things got worse when Geoff followed a vicious left to the side with a right which dropped the North Walian in the third. Up at seven, he stormed back in the fourth, perhaps feeling that his problem with the scales meant he had to get matters over quickly.

In the event, Rocky's stamina was never really tested. Pegler had the better of a toe-to-toe fifth, dominated the sixth and was landing at will in the seventh, prompting the intervention of referee Adrian Morgan. Geoff was a two-weight champion.

Manager Breen thought a British title eliminator might be forthcoming. Pegler believed he was boxing better than ever, crediting new trainer Gordon Harris with teaching him, at this late stage, how to make punches miss. But his heart was no longer in it. He never boxed again.

Geoff was briefly involved in training with Pembrokeshire guru Graham Brockway; work commitments soon put an end to that. He now works on the oil rigs in Scotland, having just one week in four in Swansea.

But when he is at home, he often shares a drink with Ray Price. "We're now the best of friends," he says. And that's as it should be.

DEAN PHILLIPS
(1976–   )

- **Commonwealth Lightweight Challenger 2004**
- **Welsh Lightweight Challenger 2007**
- **IBF Inter-Continental Super-Featherweight Challenger 1996**

Sometimes a defeat can make a boxer's name, especially if it's controversial. And when Dean Phillips put former world champion Colin McMillan on his backside for the first time in his life it raised a few eyebrows, even if referee Tony Walker somehow had the Londoner a point up when the full eight rounds were completed.

The crowd's roar of outrage signalled their disagreement, but the injustice brought the 19-year-old Llanelli boy to the attention of some influential people, notably Britain's top promoter, Frank Warren, who promptly added the unlucky loser to his regular workforce.

For all his youth, 'Dynamite' Dean was hardly inexperienced in ring matters. Father Des had introduced him to karate at five and at nine he was already a black belt. He moved on to the kick-boxing circuit, winning an array of junior tournaments culminating in a world title. He never lost in that arena.

Somehow Phillips maintained a parallel life in the orthodox code, collecting Welsh schools and youth honours, and he opted to focus on this, sparring with the likes of British champions Floyd Havard and Peter Harris while still a junior.

Dean, then a featherweight, turned pro as soon as he passed his 18th birthday,

Dean Phillips

Dean (left) faces Michael Muya

joining the Colin Breen camp. Nerves led to a debut defeat in Bristol, but a 60-second knockout of Cardiff traveller Phil Janes less than two weeks later set him back on course and there was only one setback – a half-point loss in Birmingham to the naturally bigger Andrew Maynard, later to challenge for the British lightweight title – in eight outings, which included a visit to Scotland to outscore the former Olympian and reigning British feather king Michael Deveney.

Following the showdown with McMillan and the link-up with Sports Network, Phillips found himself bidding for the IBF Inter-Continental super-feather strap. The Welshman and his Yorkshire rival, dyed-blond dustman Peter Judson, put on a tremendous show for the punters at Manchester's Bowlers Arena on September 19, 1996. There was barely a clinch as the pair hammered away at each other for the best part of 10 rounds. Dean had never before gone past eight and it was clear that the intensity and workrate was taking its toll on his defences as Judson drove home a volley which dropped the Welshman on the seat of his pants. He bravely rose, but was shipping punishment when referee Dave Parris stepped in and shepherded him back to his corner.

Shown by Sky's computer stats to have hurled 900 punches in the nine completed rounds – that works out as one every two seconds – Phillips collapsed in the ring from sheer exhaustion. After treatment he was able to descend under his own steam, but spent 48 hours in hospital for observation until scans indicated nothing to worry about.

He took a year off before returning with a win as a lightweight. An attempt to return to super-feather proved disastrous, Steve Conway clearly outpointing him in Cardiff, and Dean left the sport to focus on his studies as a computer programmer.

It was four and a half years before he reappeared – with a bang! Midlands journeyman Nigel Senior, 41 a few days earlier, had never lost inside a round in his 89 previous engagements; Phillips, scornful of the very idea of ringrust, dropped him with a left hook and then slammed home a body blow which left the Nottingham man on the deck, gazing helplessly at the colourful murals of the Brangwyn Hall.

Two further victories, a stoppage of former Commonwealth challenger Gary Hibbert and a decision over former holder Michael Muya, earned Dean his own opportunity on November 19, 2004, against ex-soldier Kevin Bennett, who had taken the belt from Kenyan Muya in Bridgend a year earlier.

Birmingham-born Bennett, whose father was from Tonyrefail, had settled in Hartlepool and had home advantage at the town's Borough Hall. Known as 'The Bulldog', he showed canine tenacity in worrying at Phillips throughout, never allowing the Llanelli man to get a foothold in the contest. Dean touched down briefly in the second – more a case of balance than genuine discomfort – and struggled with a torn pectoral muscle, but staged something of a mid-fight recovery before Kevin finished strongly to earn a 118-111 margin from referee Phil Edwards.

There was another 15 months' inactivity before Phillips was back with a two-round retirement win over Basingstoke southpaw Jon Honney at the York Hall, but disaster accompanied his next outing at the old East End venue, when Bulgarian Tontcho Tontchev, a former Olympic silver medallist and WBU champion as a pro, flattened him in half a round, referee Jeff Hinds abandoning the count so that the paramedics could administer oxygen.

There was to be one final chapter in the story. Dean was matched with Swansea's Damian Owen at Neath Sports Centre on March 2, 2007, with the vacant Welsh lightweight crown up for grabs. Owen, 10 years younger than his 31-year-old rival, set the pace while Phillips, troubled by the recurrence of a shoulder problem first experienced against Bennett, found it difficult to throw his trademark left hook.

Damian scored well with his own head shots, but it was a left downstairs sent Dean to his haunches in the fourth, a grimace in the direction of his father in the corner indicating that he was done for the night.

There were suggestions of a comeback, but it never materialised and Phillips turned his full attention to establishing his own web design business.

DELME PHILLIPS
(1947–   )

🥊 Welsh Heavyweight Challenger 1972

The Welsh-speaking youngster from Nantycaws, at 6ft 5in, was constantly described as "a giant", yet only twice, in his last year, did he weigh above what is now the cruiserweight limit. There again, only three of his opponents did. The statistics are a stark reminder of how much boxers have grown over the last four decades.

Back in the 1960s Delme Phillips was seemingly made for the ring. It was only a lack of nearby facilities that delayed his entry into the sport until his late teens, when Henry Thomas at Tumble ABC – then based in a colliery canteen at Cross Hands – guided him to a Welsh ABA final after less than a dozen contests. He lost on points to the more experienced Cardiffian, Dennis Avoth, brother of future British and Commonwealth light-heavy king Eddie. His was to prove a recurring name in Del's career.

Naturally, the professionals were watching. And Phillips threw in his lot with colourful Cardiff docker Mac Williams, which meant a move to the capital. His new mentor found him work driving a brewery lorry, with another new heavyweight recruit, Rod Parkinson – the man Del beat in the ABA semis – helping him deliver the beer.

His pro bow was nearly a disaster. Bournemouth southpaw Paul Cassidy battered the tense newcomer for the first three minutes; somehow Phillips made it to the interval, when the inimitable Mac suggested forcefully that he should try hitting back. It did the trick. Del relaxed, went out and drove Cassidy around the ring, the bell coming just as the referee seemed on the verge of intervening. No matter, a renewed onslaught in the third brought the stoppage and a hard-earned winning start.

Delme Phillips

Cassidy was beaten twice more before the year was out and, although Phillips was floored in the first before halting Jamaican Obe Hepburn, he compiled a seven-bout winning streak. That came to an end against old foe Avoth in a thriller which had the Sophia Gardens crowd on their feet; many felt Del was unlucky in having to settle for a draw from referee Joe Morgan. The West Walian was certainly one of them!

Just five days later, his unbeaten record was no more. In the first series of an open heavyweight tournament at the World Sporting Club, Phillips was outpointed over three rounds by debutant Richard Dunn. It's a result that looks better in retrospect, given that Dunn went on to claim British, Commonwealth and European titles and make a brave challenge to a peak Muhammad Ali.

Trips to Nottingham saw Del halted in two by unbeaten Don Halden and then knocked out in 64 seconds by another Midlander, Jack Cotes, but at least he lasted the course in losing to future title challenger Billy Aird.

Back on home soil things were better. A rematch with the stocky Avoth was recognised as an eliminator for the right to challenge Welsh heavyweight boss Carl Gizzi and a packed house at Swansea's Top Rank Suite cheered Phillips to a points victory after 10 combative rounds. Half a stone heavier and several inches taller, Del used his reach to keep Dennis at bay much of the time, but found himself under severe pressure late on before emerging with a half-point advantage on referee Adrian Morgan's card.

Phillips was by now a steelworker and an accident shattered his left hand, demanding a year on the sidelines. There was a positive side effect, however. Unable to practise his favoured left hook, Del focussed on developing the right – and that was the fist that flattened big Jamaican Bert Johnson on his return at Llanelli's Glen Ballroom. Two more wins helped him to that delayed shot at the national crown; Gizzi had moved on, so it was, yet again, that man Avoth on the other stool on April 24, 1972, in London, at the National Sporting Club.

Traditionally, the dinner-jacketed members do not applaud during rounds, but that rule was put to the test as the pair produced 10 rounds of non-stop action. This time Dennis forced his way inside and worked with both hands, while Del neglected his jab to go for the body as well. Tactically, that decision may have cost him the title, Adrian Morgan favouring Avoth by a quarter-point, signifying a one-round margin.

By the end of the year, Phillips had finished as an active boxer. He travelled to Johannesburg to meet future South African champion Jimmy Richards, tempted by the £500 purse – double what he normally earned – but he struggled with the altitude. He floored the local in the fifth, only for the count to be delayed until he reached a neutral corner. Richards was able to recover and three rounds later the referee rescued the exhausted Welshman.

His last outing came against fellow-countryman Mal Isaac at the Club Double Diamond, in Caerphilly. The unbeaten Brynmawr youngster broke Del's jaw in two places and he never boxed again, resuming a rugby career as a second row with Llangennech.

Returning westward, he joined the police. On his retirement in 2000, he returned to boxing and is currently a coach at Trostre ABC, doubling up as the club secretary.

Llanelli's Glen Ballroom, where Del unveiled his new right-hand power

PETRINA PHILLIPS
(1978–   )

- **British Flyweight Challenger 1994**
- **European Super-Flyweight Challenger 1995**

When Jane Couch took the Board of Control to court in 1998 and won the right for women to be licensed as boxers, it was almost irrelevant for one Welsh girl. Three years earlier, Llanelli's Petrina Phillips had faced the most popular attraction in the German ring.

Regina Halmich, a former lawyer's clerk, was a national heroine. With most of the top male fighters migrants from Eastern Europe or further afield, as a native-born product she was the undisputed queen.

Petrina Phillips (left) with father Des and siblings Dean and Ayshea

While the teenage German was already a superstar, few east of the Loughor Bridge had ever heard of her challenger. But Petrina was not lacking in combat experience. Along with big brother Dean, she had been introduced to kick-boxing at an early age by father Des. The eldest sibling, Ayshea, excelled at karate.

Petrina and Dean both won world kick-boxing titles and Dean, who had always boxed as well, fancied earning some cash. With her brother poised to turn pro as soon as he turned 18, his little sister also looked towards the orthodox code.

In her case, 16 was the qualifying age, but a little white lie saw her make her pro bow six months early, winning a three-round decision on an all-female card in Fleetwood, home town of the aforementioned Miss Couch, an interested spectator on the night.

A stoppage win over Sonia Jones in Rugby boosted the Phillips profile and she followed up with a points decision over Sandra Williams at Brighton to establish her as one of the best performers in an admittedly small field. Dad decided to link up with the Women's International Boxing Federation and stage Wales's first women-only bill at Riley's nightclub, Swansea, on September 14, 1994, with his daughter taking on Midlander Cheryll Robertson for the vacant British flyweight title.

Robertson, like most women boxers at the time – including Halmich – shared a martial arts background and had age and experience on her side. But the mother from West Bromwich found her hands full with the young Welsh girl. After eight hard rounds, the judges were unable to separate them.

Cheryll had held the WIBF European belt up at super-fly before losing it to the fast-rising Halmich, who went on to acquire the vacant world title at flyweight. Having shown herself to be at least the equal of Robertson, Petrina was soon lined up to provide the German's next victim. When she travelled to Cologne to face her at the Sartory Säle on November 4, 1995, it was Regina's continental 8st 3lb honour, which she still held, that was at stake.

The challenger had some top assistance in her preparation. Thrice-weekly trips with Dean to Dai Gardiner's Fleur-de-Lys gym brought regular sparring with Robbie Regan, a recent challenger for the WBO fly throne.

Halmich was still three weeks short of her 19th birthday, but she was two years older than the visitor from Llanelli. And her experience already included trips to Italy and to Las Vegas, where a cut cheek had resulted in what was to remain the only defeat in a 56-bout career.

After her father had won a battle to have *Hen Wlad fy Nhadau* played pre-fight, rather than *God Save the Queen* – the Germans compromised by including both – Petrina came close to handing out another loss to the girl from Karlsruhe. With Phillips constantly moving forward and Regina boxing off the back foot, it was one of those contests in which personal preference can influence the scoring.

When the 10 rounds were complete, the local heroine's right eye was virtually closed; the only scars of battle on her challenger were rope marks on her back. But the verdict went unanimously, but narrowly, in favour of the home fighter.

With Petrina a natural flyweight, there were attempts to secure a rematch with Halmich's world title at stake. When Regina's promoter, Klaus-Peter Kohl, turned up at a show in Cardiff, Des took the chance to press his daughter's case. But Kohl, well aware how close his money-making miss had come to defeat, had no interest in repeating the risk.

Regina Halmich

Halmich went on to win world titles at two more weights, while she kept the WIBF flyweight strap for another 12 years until her retirement in 2007. On the way she topped bills across Germany, drawing massive crowds, while the likes of the Klitschko brothers, Juan Carlos Gómez and Artur Grigorian appeared on her undercards.

There was an appearance as a centrefold in the German edition of *Playboy*, a live "fight" with a heavyweight male TV host – she broke his nose with a straight left – fitness DVDs and an autobiography. She remains one of the biggest celebrities in her country.

For Petrina, life has been rather different. Surgery to remove cysts left her with further problems which meant she was no longer able to train. It was a sad end to the career of Wales's best female boxer.

RAY PRICE
(1961–   )

🥊 Welsh Light-Welterweight Champion 1982–83

For a fighter named Ray to be tagged 'Sugar' may lack a little in originality. But forget Robinson and Leonard – for fight fans in Swansea there was only one 'Sugar Man'.

The tall redheaded southpaw began at 15 with the Swansea RAOB club, but switched to the Gwent gym, nearer his Townhill home. But after just 12 amateur bouts, the teenager turned pro in 1979 with Colin Breen.

No fewer than four of his first nine fights were draws, but there was only one loss. As the opposition improved, Price found things harder, four defeats in his next five including an eight-round decision as a late substitute against Welsh light-welter king Billy Vivian. The Merthyr man retired later in the year and Price found himself contesting the vacant throne with local rival and stablemate Geoff Pegler at the Top Rank Suite on March 22, 1982.

Price, in the middle of a split with Breen, was forced to watch his titular manager working in the opposite corner. In addition, Geoff was on a four-fight unbeaten run, while Ray's last outing had seen him stopped in 93 seconds by Liverpool's Robbie Robinson.

Pegler started fast, targeting Price's body, but Ray absorbed the early onslaught and gradually began to impose his jab as well as landing sharp counters. At the start of the final session, Price was rocked and looked in some difficulty, only to turn the tables and stagger Pegler as the fans roared. At the end of a cracking contest, Cardiff referee Jim Brimmell had Ray ahead by three rounds.

By the time they met again Price was managed by burly Midlander Ron Gray, but once again coming off a first-round hammering, this time by

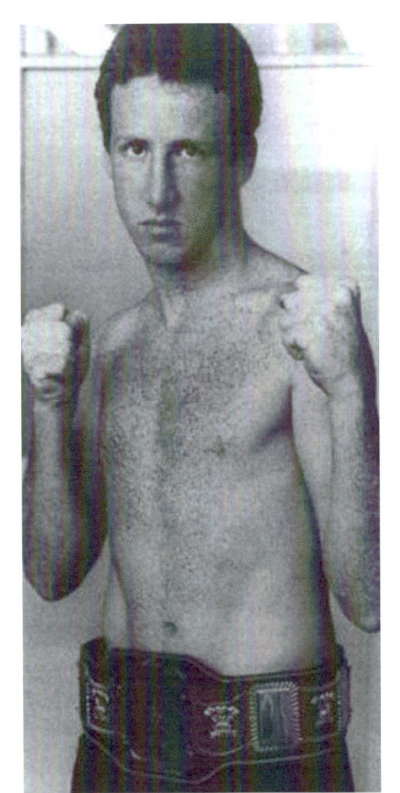

Ray Price

Londoner Gunther Roomes. And the Welsh title affair, on May 27, 1983, also ended after just one episode – but not in the same fashion.

By now the boxers were sworn enemies, each with a large band of followers. There had been frequent incidents around the city and it was no great surprise when trouble broke out at the Top Rank. Sporadic skirmishes turned into a full-blown riot and the show had to be abandoned after just three minutes of the main event.

The clash was eventually rearranged for the city's Dolphin Hotel, where it was felt security would be easier to maintain, on December 19, 1983. Price took control early, keeping on the move and firing out left leads, with Pegler slow to get into the fight. Geoff hurt Ray with a left to the body in the fourth, and although the holder took the fifth, the sixth saw his gumshield knocked out as he came under increased pressure.

Price tried to keep matters at distance, but the stocky Pegler was now in charge, rocking his man early in the eighth. Later in the round Ray emerged from a close-quarters exchange with a cut near his right eye and when he attacked in desperation it resulted in a further clash of heads in the closing seconds. Back in the corner, it took only one look for Price's seconds to pull their man out.

Pegler soon moved up to welterweight and when it came to deciding his successor, Price was paired with another Swansea man, Michael Harris, at the Afan Lido on June 13, 1984. Harris, just 19, had lost only once in 14 pro outings and was tipped to go far. But he found Price a tough nut to crack. The former champion, though still only 22, had a fair few ring miles on the clock, and "old-manned" him in the early sessions. His close-quarter work, often involving an errant shoulder, hustled Mike out of his usual rhythm, a swelling beneath his left eye evidence of Ray's attentions.

Harris gradually began to settle, making Price miss while landing more of his own shots and bringing blood from Ray's nose. When the final bell sounded, there was only half-a-point between them on referee Ivor Bassett's card – but it was in Harris's favour.

It looked to be the beginning of the end for 'Sugar'. He won only one of his next five, but Breen – the pair were now reconciled – reckoned he could get a match with Pembrokeshire's Steve Davies for the Welsh light-middle crown. When Davies defended against another Swansea fighter, John McGlynn, Price was at ringside with a view to challenging the winner. Then fate took a hand: Ray slipped, fell down the Patti Pavilion steps and fractured a vertebra. Forced to hang up his gloves, he became an assistant trainer in the Breen gym – and one of the men he looked after was his conqueror, Mike Harris.

There was to be a late twist in the tale. Nearly seven years on, a fit-again Price launched a comeback, joining the select few who have boxed in three decades. And Harris, whose own career had by now run its course, was the man chosen to train his former mentor!

For Ray, now a middleweight, the return was brief, two stoppage losses hurrying him into permanent retirement. Since then, the 'Sugar Man' has earned a crust in the carpet-fitting trade he has followed since school. Boxing, on the other hand, has played no part in his life.

CHRIS WARE
(1982–)

Welsh Middleweight Champion 2015–

The phone call came at midday. Can you get over to Bristol tonight? Frankie Borg's opponent has dropped out – will you fill in?

Owning your own gym means you are fit for action at any time. Chris Ware, proprietor of the Ware-House just off Swansea's Kingsway, jumped at the opportunity to have a crack at the Welsh middleweight champion, albeit over just four rounds.

As an amateur with Bonymaen, Chris, with Enzo Maccarinelli in the corner, had won a Welsh ABA title in his 10th contest, taking the 2009 light-heavyweight honour with a clear win over Newport's Lee Churcher, later a national pro champion. In the semi-final he had beaten Frankie on a double countback. They had sparred on occasion since. Now it was for real.

After four straight wins as a pro with Paul Boyce and trainer Rocky Reynolds – they included a demolition job on debutant Simon Parkins which convinced the Portsmouth lad to abort his career after less than three minutes – Ware took two years out before returning with new manager Gary Lockett and John Kaighin calling the shots in the corner.

His comeback began shakily with a rusty points loss in Merthyr against Aberdare newcomer Morgan Jones, another boasting a Welsh amateur crown. But in the short-notice encounter with Borg the impact was immediate: a right dropped the Cardiffian in the opener and another knockdown in the last guaranteed the late sub a shock verdict.

Promoter Chris Sanigar quickly rematched the duo for his Newport

Chris Ware

Centre card on March 13, 2015, with the title at stake. The lesson of the first meeting was reinforced: Frankie was the better boxer, Ware had the power. It proved an intriguing contest.

The first, third, fourth and seventh saw Borg on the canvas, but the shaven-headed holder won the three rounds in which he stayed on his feet. The two-point sessions meant Ware, barring a reversal of everything demonstrated by their two meetings, was destined for victory.

In the event, the sums were academic. The fourth knockdown prompted referee Reece Carter to dispense with the count and wave it off, one second before the gong to end the seventh. The belt was heading to the Mumbles.

TOBIAS WEBB
(1988–)

- Welsh Super-Middleweight Champion 2013–
- WBC International Super-Middleweight Challenger 2014

When Mario Maccarinelli turned up to press conferences featuring son Enzo, there would invariably be a youngster with him. And Mario would always make a point of stressing that the boy would be the next champion in the family.

Alas, Mario was not to live long enough to see his prophesy fulfilled. The Italian-born trainer died 13 months before his grandson claimed his first belt. Although, bizarrely, none of the paying punters knew he had won it.

Tobias Lucca Webb first laced up the gloves as a nine-year-old at Bonymaen ABC, the Swansea club founded by his grandfather, and collected a string of national honours, including a senior ABA title, before turning pro with Enzo Calzaghe early in 2009.

He enjoyed a fine start in the paid ranks, but a shot at the popular Prizefighter tournament produced mixed results. Victories over veteran former world champion Robin Reid and once-beaten Midlander Jahmaine Smyle took him to the final, but at a cost. Both contests had been gruelling affairs, while future Commonwealth champion Rocky Fielding had stopped both his rivals and was comparatively fresh; twice he floored the exhausted Welshman, who was pulled out at the end of the first.

Tobias, now with Paul Boyce, picked up a few wins on his new manager's promotions and was rewarded with a shot at the vacant Welsh 12st title at Swansea's Oceana nightclub on March 2, 2013.

Tobias Webb

Tobias on the attack against Lewis Patterson

Eyebrows were raised when the area council accepted Lewis Patterson as co-challenger, given that the Cardiffian had only three fights to his name and had lost one of those.

But Patterson defied his critics with an impressive start, dominating the early stages, although Webb was beginning to make his own presence felt by the end of the fourth, when confusion and chaos took over. Lewis's chief second, Tony Borg, called referee Wynford Jones over to tell him that his man had damaged his left hand and could not continue. Jones ruled a Technical Draw and this was announced to the crowd.

However, that rule applies only to injuries caused by accidental foul play – usually a cut caused by a head clash – and, as the disappointed fans dispersed, ringside officials pondered the situation. After much animated discussion and a phone call to Board secretary Robert Smith, steward-in-charge Ron Pavett ruled that Patterson's retirement meant Webb was the winner. The new champion was informed in his dressing-room and presented with the belt in a hurriedly arranged ceremony in one of the club's bars.

Tobias picked up a couple more wins, although a perceived lack of dedication and a tendency to coast when bouts did not motivate him brought a split from Boyce. Big guns Matchroom were still keen, though, and boss Eddie Hearn offered him a shot at British titleholder Paul Smith, only for the Board to veto it. An alternative plan to pair them for the vacant WBO Inter-Continental strap fell through when Smith cried off with an elbow injury.

In the event, it was the youngest of the four fighting Smiths, Callum, who faced Webb at Cardiff's Motorpoint Arena on May 17, 2014, with the Scouser's WBC International honour at stake. Unlike Callum's previous foes, the Swansea boy, who had been sparring in Germany with world ruler Arthur Abraham, took the fight to him, his jab earning him the first round. But in the second the 6ft 3in Smith switched his target to the body, flooring Webb three times to claim his ninth successive stoppage.

Despite the loss Webb was matched with Liam Cameron in a British title eliminator, though he had to travel to his rival's Sheffield backyard. The southpaw local kept Tobias on the end of his jab for much of the fight – despite damaging his right early in the encounter – and, although the Welshman had some success in the middle rounds, Liam re-established control and coasted to victory by margins of three, four and five points.

JIM WILDE
(1911–1990)

Welsh Heavyweight Champion 1935–1936

The whole world knew who Jimmy Wilde was. Even today, the greatest flyweight who ever lived is revered well beyond these shores. But there was another champion of the same name who is held in similar respect in Swansea.

Physically as different from his namesake as is humanly possible, 'Big Jim' was a hero not merely for what he achieved in boxing, but for his actions when the British Union of Fascists visited the city's Plaza cinema in 1934. The imposing Wilde had been approached to look after the security of their leader, Oswald Mosley. They asked the wrong man.

After Mosley had delivered an anti-Semitic tirade, he began to answer questions submitted earlier. "I work for a Jew," read the first. "Should I change my employer?" Mosley was unequivocal. "I can't understand why anyone would work for a Jew. Find a new job," he insisted.

At that point the questioner stood, his clerical collar visible to all. It was the Rev. Leon Atkin, a popular Congregationalist minister. Bedlam broke out. Mosley was rushed away, screaming, "Blasphemy!" Wilde, who had been sitting next to the clergyman, led the charge and the Blackshirts were driven from the building.

Things were not always as exciting in the ring, but Jim had his moments. The Port Tennant youngster's record was decent, if unspectacular, until 1935, which he began with praiseworthy wins over Midlander Frank Borrington and Scot Steve McCall and earned a shot at the vacant Welsh heavyweight title against Charlie Bundy, someone he had already beaten on cuts.

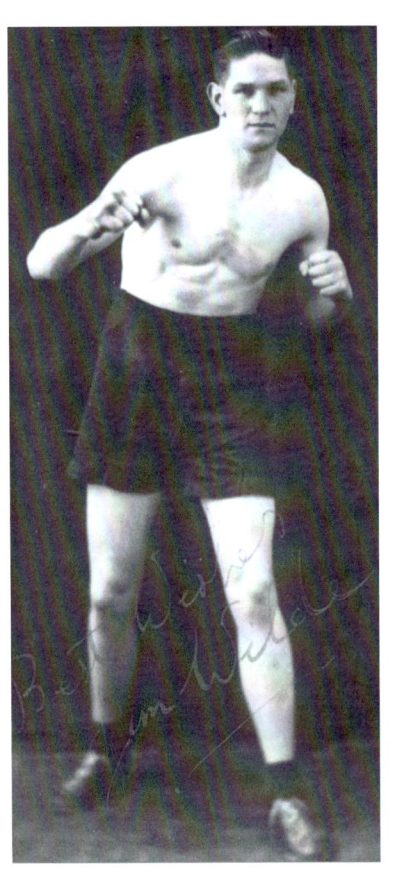

Jim Wilde

The Rhondda man had twice challenged unsuccessfully for the light-heavy honour and missed out again at the Mannesmann Hall on June 8, 1935. The shorter Bundy tried in vain to fight in close, but Jim's long left arm maintained the distance he needed to control the action. Once Wilde adopted the uppercut as an effective weapon against a stocky foe there was little doubt about the outcome.

He kept his winning streak going throughout the year, although fortunate to escape early defeat at the Vetch against an Egyptian visitor, Salah El Din, making his first appearance in a British ring. The five-figure crowd were impressed by the newcomer's physique and then by his power, which saw Jim on the deck three times in the opener and again early in the second. But, just as disaster seemed inevitable, the local hero rediscovered his boxing ability, the muscular Din tired and the sixth saw a series of body shots force the visitor to give in.

Once Tommy Farr abandoned his light-heavyweight ambitions and joined the big boys, a meeting was inevitable. Wilde was given a controversial draw – despite flooring the Rhondda fighter in the fourth, he was under fire throughout – and a rematch was arranged for Jim's belt, while also recognised as a British title eliminator.

More than 15,000 at the Vetch on September 14, 1936, witnessed the passing of the baton. After a slow start, the contest soon developed into a proper ding-dong, each scoring effectively. The holder – by now training in a gym he and his father built at St Thomas – was dropped by a body shot in the third and was also troubled by a swollen left eye, but was still competitive until the seventh, when a right to the midriff sent him down for the full count.

Wilde was now moving in decent company, although losing to reigning British light-heavy boss Eddie Phillips, Californian Buddy Baer – brother of the charismatic Max – and future British heavy king Jack London.

Farr relinquished the Welsh honour on winning the Lonsdale Belt and Jim was matched with Ebbw Vale prospect George James for the vacant throne on February 21,

Jim Wilde with his nephews, aged four and five

1938, before 10,000 enthusiastic fans at the Mountain Ash Pavilion. Wilde suffered damage to his left eye in the second and within two rounds the swelling had left him virtually blind on that side. With a stone advantage, he ignored the handicap and came close to stopping George in the 10th, but as he tired his punches became lower and he was finally disqualified barely a minute before the scheduled final bell.

The pair met again on July 24, 1939, at a packed Mannesmann Hall. Wilde set the early pace, but an old cut reopened in the fourth and the pattern changed. James dropped him in the fifth and repeated the dose in the 11th, at which point Jim, bleeding heavily, turned to his corner, signalling that he could not see, and the towel came floating in.

He boxed sporadically for another seven years, but with little success: future world light-heavy champion Freddie Mills knocked him out early, while London twice repeated his previous stoppage. Towards the end of the war, he ran a social club in Alexandra Road, with a gym attached; one of the GIs to use it was a young Rocky Marciano.

'Big Jim' may never have hit the heights his American visitor was to achieve. But he was a worthy champion of Wales and, on one memorable occasion, a standard bearer in the battle against bigotry.

JASON WILLIAMS
(1974–   )

Welsh Welterweight Champion 2003–04

For most boxers, winning a first title is a stepping stone to bigger things. For Leon Jason Williams, it was to be the last time his arm was raised.

An outstanding junior – he won four Welsh schoolboy championships and two at youth level, twice progressing to British success – the lad from Fforestfach also struck gold and silver at the Gaelic Games, while his victory over future pro Anthony Ivy clinched a 5-5 draw for Wales Schools against the US Juniors.

Graduating to the seniors, he wore the colours of Gwent ABC to a Welsh ABA title at his first try, but was unable to repeat it in four further attempts, twice being forced to pull out through injury. It was time to turn pro and he linked up with Bristol-based manager Chris Sanigar, while amateur mentor Terry Grey looked after the training side.

Things did not start well, Plymouth journeyman Jon Harrison taking something of a hometown decision by half a point. But his next dozen bouts all ended in triumph, including revenge when Williams broke Harrison's nose and beat him in two rounds. Younger brother Darren often appeared on the same bills and, more often than not, was able to share in the celebrations.

When Jason was matched with Michael Smyth at Merthyr's Rhydycar Sports Centre on September 24, 1999, with the vacant Welsh welter belt up for grabs, there were many tipping him to return to Swansea as champion. Sure, the 'Barry Bomber' had moved in more exalted circles, contesting British and Commonwealth belts, but he was

Jason Williams

coming off a one-round hammering from Neil Sinclair in Belfast and had briefly announced his retirement.

On a show promoted by South African-based Golden Fists – their countryman, Sebastiaan Rothmann, captured the WBU cruiser belt in the main event – Williams duly dominated the first two sessions, his stylish boxing controlling things against someone whose mind seemed elsewhere. When the bell ended the second, Smyth seemed in a mood to pull out, but manager Dai Gardiner would hear none of it, pushing him back into action.

It was as well they did. Refocussed on the matter at hand, Michael began to force Jason back for the first time. And when the Swansea man missed with a right uppercut, Smyth uncorked a left which shook him down to his toes. Still wobbling, Williams tried to cling on, but Michael would not be denied. If it was a push which ultimately sent him to the canvas, there was no questioning the power in the punches that then drove Jason to his corner, where referee Ivor Bassett jumped in to the rescue.

There were two further stoppage defeats to come, against London-based Frenchman Karim Bouali and former victim Mark Ramsey, before Jason contested a belt once more. It was one of the fairly meaningless British Masters trophies, up at light-middle, which was at stake when the Welshman went to Birmingham as a late substitute to face local traveller Jimmy Vincent.

The diners at the charity show saw a thriller, with Vincent's attacks bringing blood from Williams's nose early on and cutting his left eyebrow in the fourth. But Jason came on in the second half of the 10-rounder, although he had to survive a corner inspection of that wounded optic. Jimmy recovered well in the finishing straight to clinch a somewhat generous 97-93 verdict from referee John Coyle.

When British-based Congolese Charden Ansoula knocked him out five months later, Williams disappeared from the scene and many doubted he would fight again. Yet he returned to become his nation's champion.

He had been inactive for almost a year when he faced Welsh welter king Keith Jones at the arts centre on the campus of Aberystwyth University on February 23, 2003, the first pro show in the Cardigan Bay resort for 47 years. Cefn Hengoed's Jones was a journeyman who had won only nine of his 83 fights, but they did include a shock four-round stoppage of local favourite Ross McCord in Swansea five months earlier to claim the title.

The challenger's preparation had been disrupted by a bout of chicken pox and the arrival of son Keenan, but it made little difference. Keeping exchanges at long-range, the taller Williams, now trained by Peter Harris, was in command from the first bell. The determined Jones dug deep to score to the body in the middle rounds, but he was unable to sustain it and Roddy Evans's card, a slightly wide 99-94, confirmed that the belt had changed hands.

It was a last hurrah, however, for Jason. Former British champion Derek Roche stopped him in two, future Commonwealth light-middle challenger Marcus Portman and a former holder of that honour, Michael Jones, each won on points and, finally, James Hare – another ex-Commonwealth ruler – floored and finished him in two at Bridgend Leisure Centre, referee Wynford Jones's intervention, it transpired, ending Williams's career.

These days he works as a quality control manager at the T & G Davies bakery in Mumbles and has no connection with boxing.

TAFFY WILLIAMS
(1920–1992)

Welsh Welterweight Champion 1939–1940

Taffy Williams is not a name to make its owner stand out among the boxers of Wales. And if he'd stuck to William McVeigh, the name on his birth certificate, he would have been one of a kind.

But bear in mind that the Swansea boy was in Scotland at the time he adopted his new identity. Having signed up with the Royal Scots Fusiliers, he found himself at the Redford Barracks in Edinburgh, where he soon made an impression as a sportsman. A good enough footballer to be offered terms by St Johnstone, he nevertheless opted for boxing as a supplementary source of income.

With many of his early bouts in the seaside resort of Portobello – where the young Sean Connery worked as a lifeguard – Williams soon had such a formidable reputation that finding suitable opponents became a problem and Taffy headed south to Liverpool to face his first Welsh opponent, though Tommy Jones was also an exile, having left his Pentre home to make his name in Derby. After 10 thrilling rounds, referee Jack Dare gave the nod to Williams. Stadium boss Johnny Best was suitably impressed and elevated Taffy to bill-topping status the following month. He let nobody down, outpointing Lionel Gibbs, the champion of British Guiana, in one of fiercest fights seen on Merseyside in many a year.

When Williams returned to his home town to face Billy 'Ducks' Jones, the Rhondda boy was turfed out inside a round for punching low. At least the locals were entertained by Taffy's strange routine at the weigh-in: presumably believing it might save him a few ounces, he would hold his breath, clasp his hands tightly by his chest and arch his back until he was staring up at the ceiling. There is no evidence it made any difference!

But the Swansea man's unbeaten run should have ended in Glasgow, where even he considered Frank Rice had outpointed him, only for the referee to disagree. He was also considered fortunate on his London debut to get the nod over West Indian Lefty 'Satan' Flynn.

But before the year was out he was the welterweight champion of Wales. At the Mannesmann Hall on December 4, 1939, he took on the former lightweight titleholder, George Reynolds, for the welter honour given up by Reynolds's fellow Cardiffian, Johnny Houlston.

Williams, though renowned as a banger, was also a skilful boxer and it was his left lead that won him the belt. Reynolds preferred to work inside and had his moments of success to the body, but was usually on the receiving end. The constant pummelling began to wear George down and he took a count of eight in the 12th, spending much of the session draped over the ropes. He survived and fought doggedly in the closing rounds, but Taffy was a clear winner on Ben Hardwicke's card.

Within two months he had relinquished the title, claiming he could no longer make 10st 7lb. And soon his proud unbeaten record was history. His troublesome right thumb gave out early on against Bob McLuckie, whom he had outpointed three times. But that was not responsible for the Scot scoring a first-round knockdown, nor, after Taffy had used his left to establish a lead, did it explain a further visit to the deck late in the eighth. A short right to the chin provided the exclamation mark a round later.

Taffy Williams

There was a second loss next time out, although Williams did go the distance with big-hitting Londoner George Odwell, while British champion Ernie Roderick flattened him in two rounds of a non-title encounter.

The war meant Taffy, now in the RAF, saw little ring action over the next five years, although in 1944 he took part in an inter-services tournament, for amateurs and pros, in the Brancaccio Theatre in Rome, freed by Allied forces a few months earlier. Leading Aircraftman McVeigh competed at middleweight and lost a controversial decision to an American sergeant, Ralph Burley. When he watched the final, Taffy stopped complaining about the verdict: Burley was wiped out by a French sailor, future world champion Marcel Cerdan!

Back in his birthplace, Williams faced crosstown rival Willie Piper in an official eliminator for a shot at middleweight boss Tommy Davies. In pouring rain at the Vetch Field, the prodigal son floored Willie three times in the ninth – the first from a body shot, the others from hooks – and at the end of the round Piper's tune was over.

Now managed by the mercurial Billy 'Kid' Hughes, Taffy suffered what might have been a setback when he was outpointed by former victim Tommy Jones in Trealaw, but Jones was now the Northern Area champion, which meant he could not contest the Welsh honour. Indeed, Jones was to beat Davies as well, before Williams went in with the champion on June 11, 1946.

He had drawn with the Cwmgors man the previous year, many considering the result favoured Tommy, and had been demanding a title rematch ever since. But Davies never allowed Taffy to settle and a right near the end of the first shook him, bringing blood from his nose. It was a clash at close-quarters in the second which caused the decisive injury, however, Williams pulling away with a red stream leaking from a wound on his left cheek. The damage became worse and at the end of the fourth Taffy abandoned the unequal struggle.

Matters were equally one-sided when Williams took on Vince Hawkins in Merthyr. The Hampshire man, who won the British middle crown two months later, forced a stoppage in the eighth and last round. For Williams, that was pretty much that.

SUPPORTING CAST

As ever, there are many other characters who have contributed, inside and outside the ropes, to the story of boxing in the area.

Promoters, for example, are often derided, but without their willingness to take the financial risk the fight game would never have graduated from the mountainsides. Even the booths needed a figurehead to run them, often drawn from pugilists such as William Samuels, who still paraded their own skills to bring in the punters.

A publican's son, "Billy Sam" was already middle-aged when he earned £100, a big sum in those days, for lasting three rounds with world heavyweight champion John L. Sullivan. Back in his teenage years, Billy had been a travelling sparmate of John Camel Heenan, the American remembered for his epic battle with Herefordshire's Tom Sayers.

As the sport became more respectable, businessmen became involved and brought some imagination to the proceedings. The legendary Jim Driscoll called Swansea's J.T. Jones "the cleverest in the business" after he boosted flagging ticket sales for one show by hiring someone to stick a poster on the face of the town hall clock.

Swans' star Jack Fowler promoted boxing ...

... while the club's Vetch Field home hosted the sport

Trevor Wignall

Some crossed from other fields: Welsh international centre-forward Jack Fowler, top scorer when Swansea Town won the Third Division (South) in 1924-25, became a fight promoter a few years later, staging shows at the Shaftesbury Hall while still on the club's books.

It was not an all-male preserve, either. The diminutive Teresa Breen put on many a bout in the late 1980s, memorably appearing in a leprechaun's outfit when one of husband Colin's fighters, Terry Magee, boxed for the Irish title.

In fact, there has been significant female input in West Walian boxing. In 1994, 22-year-old Melanie Lewis, from Llanelli, became the first woman to take out a second's licence, helping manager Glynne Davies in the corner. Joanne Bromfield, daughter of respected trainer Jim, having started as an eight-year-old massaging Frank McCord's shoulders, became a physio working with several pros and the Welsh and Irish national amateur squads.

There have always been links between boxing and the arts. Mal Pope, from Brynhyfryd, contributed *Contender*, a musical based on the career of heavyweight legend Tommy Farr. As for wordsmiths, Trevor Wignall, from Llangyfelach, doubled as novelist and Britain's highest-paid sports writer.

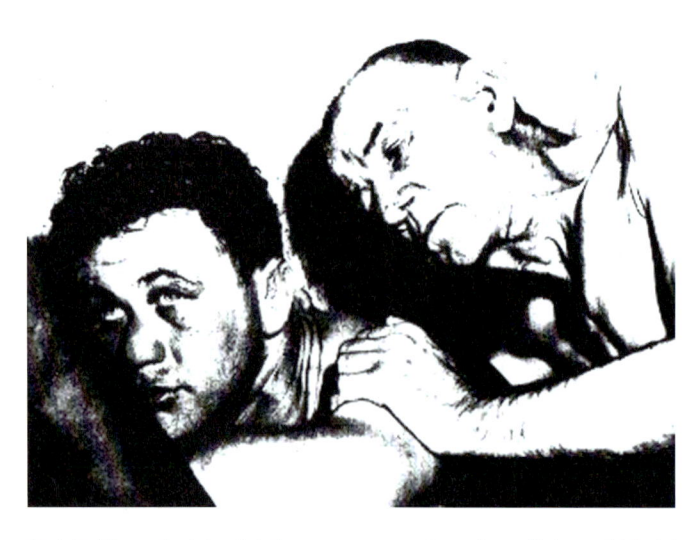

He fell in love with boxing through watching Dick Ambrose, a local docker who took on all and sundry in the 1890s.

These days pundits laud the skills of such trainers as Freddie Roach and the late Emanuel Steward, but early last century there was nobody to match Dai Dollings. A bare-knuckle battler in his youth, the Swansea man travelled the world as a fight guru before settling in New York, where he guided

Dai Dollings, in his eighties, massages American fighter Al Reid

SUPPORTING CAST

Gareth Howells

many a top name as well as teaching the ropes to future Hall of Fame cornerman Ray Arcel. Dai, who also claimed he could cure baldness, was still working in his eighties.

So, more recently, was Gareth Howells. His reputation may not have spanned the Atlantic, but the man from Llangennech helped found Trostre ABC and was a trainer there for more than 70 years, right up to his death, aged 87, in 2013. A much deserved MBE came his way in 2008. A decade earlier he had appeared as a referee in the film *Up'n'Under*, in a scene which saw Llanelli sisters Petrina and Ayshea Phillips swapping the punches.

A Swansea man took a silver medal in the 1938 Empire Games, but – like Brian Curvis two decades later – Morry Dennis, a student in London, did so in an England vest. Perhaps he gained some consolation from the fact that his conqueror in the final was Cardiffian Denis Reardon, winning Wales's first-ever gold.

Another top amateur was Nigel Page, who once took Barry McGuigan to a majority decision when even the Ulsterman thought he had lost. Page will always be remembered in Swansea as the driving force behind the

Morry Dennis

167

THE BOXERS OF WALES – SWANSEA & LLANELLI

Nigel Page

annual Kilvey Hill run, in which competitors race while carrying bags of cement. The charity event, won several times by former world champion Enzo Maccarinelli, was started after Nigel's baby daughter almost died in infancy. Alas, Nigel himself was killed in a fall from a roof while at work; the run continues in his memory.

The second city's greatest-ever sportsman might also have been a boxer. John Charles gloved up as a youngster under the supervision of Dai Curvis and while on National Service became Northern Command heavy champion. Jack Solomons made him an offer to turn pro, but he stuck to football.

Not to worry, though. Even without 'The Gentle Giant', Swansea and Llanelli have produced more than their share of heroes in the ring.

BIBLIOGRAPHY

The following are among many publications consulted during the writing of this book:
Sporting Life, Mirror of Life, Boxing, Boxing News, Boxing Monthly, Western Mail, South Wales Echo, South Wales Daily News, South Wales Evening Post, Llanelli Star.
Wales and its Boxers, ed. Peter Stead and Gareth Williams (University of Wales)
Swansea Boxers, by Jeff Burns (Dinefwr)
All in my Corner, by Tony Lee (TL Associates)
Slings and Arrows, by John Davies (Paragon)
The following websites were also useful sources of information:
boxrec.com, Welsh Warriors, www.boxinghistory.org.uk, Amateur Boxing Results, Rootschat, Rootsweb, Ancestry, Find My Past.

St David's Press
Also by Gareth Jones

THE BOXERS OF WALES
CARDIFF

"Some of the greatest boxers in Britain have come out of Cardiff and this book is a must read for fight fans, whether you're Welsh or not." *Colin Hart, The Sun*

"This book is not just about the famous fighters, it's about the forgotten heroes."
Steve Bunce, Boxing Broadcaster & Journalist

"A compelling and fascinating study." *Claude Abrams, Editor, Boxing News*

"Boxing fans in and out of Wales will love this collection of mini biographies profiling no less than 50 classic boxers from the Cardiff area...An indispensable guide to Cardiff boxers and a great resource for compiling those pub quizzes!"
South Wales Argus

"...a long overdue reminder of how much Cardiff has given to boxing. The verdict? A knockout" *Dan O'Neill, South Wales Echo*

978-1-902719-26-9   160pp   £14.99   PB

THE BOXERS OF WALES
MERTHYR
ABERDARE & PONTYPRIDD

"masterpiece... a must-read for any boxing fan...Compelling stuff."
Steve Lillis, News of the World

"The Valleys of South Wales have produced many fighters known worldwide ... but this book reminds us that there were others who lit up the ring in their day."
Gareth A. Davies, Daily Telegraph

"For generations of Merthyr's youth, boxing has been as much a means of self-expression as a way out of grinding poverty. This book does full justice to a sporting tradition that has shaped the town's character and given the world some unforgettable champions." *Mario Basini, Author, 'Real Merthyr'*

978-1-902719-29-0   160pp   £14.99   PB

THE BOXERS OF WALES
RHONDDA

"When Boxing News marked its centenary in 2009 by choosing the best British boxer of the previous 100 years, we opted for the one and only Jimmy Wilde. But the Rhondda produced many other outstanding fighters, as this book reminds us."
Tris Dixon, Editor, Boxing News

"When it comes to in-depth research, they don't come much better than Gareth Jones - as his latest tome perfectly illustrates, with a trawl through the Rhondda's staggering boxing history. The likes of the great Tommy Farr and Jimmy Wilde get the Jones treatment, along with a host of tales surrounding so many boxers from this mining area that produced such a rich seam of boxing greats."
Kevin Francis, Boxing Correspondent, Daily Star

978-1-902719-33-7   160pp   £14.99   PB

DRAGONS vs EAGLES
Wales vs. America
in the Boxing Ring

"The epic battles between Welsh and American fighters provide the author with an abundant harvest for this book. All the historic clashes are featured, but unquestionably the greatest - Tommy Farr's gallant defeat against Joe Louis - understandably takes pride of place. Gareth Jones doesn't let his readers down, also highlighting Jim Driscoll, Freddie Welsh, Colin Jones and Joe Calzaghe among others whose wars with men from across the Atlantic are part of Wales's sporting folklore." *Colin Hart, Boxing Columnist, The Sun*

978-1-902719-382   176pp   £14.99   PB

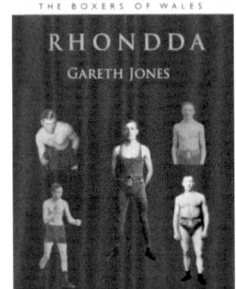